M000288877

Prison Letters: Walking To Honor

by

Veracruz Pedroza Sanchez

Letters by

Fernando Julio Sanchez

Read, rise, & inspire!

Copyright © 2013 by Veracruz Pedroza Sanchez

All rights reserved.

Cover design by Glory Sanchez
Book design by Veracruz Pedroza Sanchez

No part of this book may be reproduced in any form or by any electronic or
mechanical means including information storage and retrieval systems,
without permission in writing from the author. The only exception is by a
reviewer, who may quote short excerpts in a review. This book is a partial
work of fiction. Some names, characters, places, and incidents either are
products of the author's imagination or are used fictitiously. Any
resemblance to actual persons, living or dead, events, or locales
is entirely coincidental.
Published by Lightning Source, a subsidiary of Ingram Press Publishers
Available through Ingram Press, and available for order through Ingram
Press Catalogues
Visit my website at www.verasanchez.com

Printed in the United States of America

First Printing: October 2013

ISBN 978-0615818153
Ebook ISBN 978-1-62747-018-6
LCN Pending

I dedicate this book to my mother and father.
Thank you for allowing me to fail and bounce back
because of your love and support.

In memory of
Josefina Moroyoqui Sanchez
Ramon Sanchez
Ralph "Cuco" Pedroza
Michael Pedroza
Anthony Ortiz
Nina Ortiz

Preface

Take a moment to close your eyes, and visualize someone special. It can be anyone. When you open them, who did you see? For me, I see my father. He was there for me growing up, supporting me when I made wrong decisions, and I have made many. My dad was at every basketball game, whether I played or coached them. He was at every track meet, too. The next day, at school, students would come up to me and ask about my dad. When I bump into old friends or acquaintances from high school, they ask how my dad is doing, and I reply, "He's the same." The school administration would call my Uncle Chunky's house to see if my dad was going to the high school games in order to beef up security. He was *the* loudest, to say it lightly. He said it was because I made him proud.

I do not know if Nando ever had that feeling of someone being proud of him. My guess is no. I do not think anyone ever said those words to him, "I'm proud of you." Through his letters, the reader will see an insight, an insight that I did not fabricate or use my words to portray as his. Nando was a very talented writer, among other things in which the reader will soon experience. He loved animals, had a pet lizard he got for Christmas that kept him company. He also had a turtle, cats, and a few dogs throughout his life.

Nando had a lot of nicknames that were given to him by many family members, mainly my dad. When he was little, Nando use to watch the Ninja Turtles. Actually, we all did. For his birthday, he was given a large Ninja Turtle stuffed animal. It was "Donatello." My dad nicknamed him, "Donatello, Donatello, everybody's favorite fellow." Then, there was "Lil' Child." My dad gave him this name too, because he was the youngest, and he wrote him a poem: "Little Child, Little Child, smile for a while, little child." Before my grandma had passed away, she had named Nando "El Terror" because he was always up to something mischievous. Tio Rick named him "Waldo" because he was always missing. It was in reference to the "Where's Waldo?" books.

Nando's troubles began in junior high when he started to disappear for days at a time. Nobody took the time to search for him. When I was at my Uncle Chunky's house, Nando was walking down the street. He had been gone for a few days. Monchi, his oldest brother, was upset. He grabbed Nando by the back of his shirt and dragged him in the house. I don't know what happened or the talk they had. The door was shut, and I was standing outside. I do not know where he went or who he had been with. I am not sure if anyone knew because when he was questioned, he did not answer. Nando was in and out of jail, and then jail eventually became prison. Many family members expected this from him, expected him to go back in once he came out. And he did. He was not stupid. He knew the consequences of his actions. I often wondered if he purposely chose to go back to prison.

His last time out, as a free man, the cops surrounded Uncle Chunky's truck, pointed their guns and had everyone come out and lie on the street. Nando was on parole at the time, and that is when he was sentenced to five years in prison for possession of drugs. The last time we were together, we went bar hopping at local dive bars in downtown with his sisters, brothers, and Uncle Chunky. We had a lot of fun, laughing, sharing stories, clinging our beer mugs, and tequila shots, *salud*. At the end of the night, I took Nando's hand and danced with him in the streets, showing him some ballet folklorico steps my dad taught me when I was a little girl.

To the reader, I share not only the stories of Nando and me growing up, but the relationship Nando had with the rest of our family. His letters were written over a four-year period, letters I still have and hold dear. Our book is a combination of two voices, two different points of view on life, hardships, redemption, mistakes, forgiveness, and change. Nando paints himself as a person, not a felon, as society placed that label on him. Nando will always be missed, always be loved. With our book, Nando makes me proud. I hope you feel the same way.

The Red House

Playing hide-n-seek is always one of my favorite games, even if it requires running around in public places or other people's property. Nana and Tata live in a modest red house, with air tasting of homemade tortillas and cigar boxes. The older grandkids built a swing out of an old junkyard tire that firmly meshes around a peppertree, and the rope tangled in the hair of those girls who didn't comb their ponytail. I am the prime candidate for this sticky situation. The first time I got my hair in a mess, my dad wobbled over with the rusty clippers in his hands, yanked my braid in the opposite direction of the swing, and chopped at my naps. The front steps of the red house lead to the dim lighting of a quiet living room, with a single, narrow hallway that connects to a kitchen, a couple of bedrooms, and a bathroom with a small window that's just big enough for me to jump on my dad's shoulders and squeeze through every time he misplaces his keys. As the hallway reaches the back of the house, the sounds became more apparent.

My dad holds a Miller Lite can and laughs rowdily as he explains how he's been around the block more than the ice cream truck. He catches me observing him from the back door and waves me over. I sigh and drag my feet to stall because he'll spend countless minutes introducing me to relatives I don't know yet when I would rather be playing with my cousins. I swindle through a crowd of adults who sing along to the live music of my uncles' band. Tio Rick heavily plucks the upright bass and spins it around, not missing a beat for the upcoming tune, while Uncle Chunky, in a husky voice, sings in two different languages. When he forgets the words in Spanish, he'll replace it with an English one, the impractical usage of bilingualism.

"Is this your daughter? She is so big now. I remember her when she was just a baby," Cousin Imelda reminisces. "She's a pretty little girl," she adds, her voice raspy and cold, like the winter nights. She bends down to caress the top of my head while holding a lit cigarette and a beer can in the same hand. The tags from her yellow spaghetti tank top stick out from the back, and her *nalgas* sag from underneath her gray cotton miniskirt as she bends over to kiss me, leaving a bright pink lip print on my cheek.

"I may not be pretty, but I'm good," my dad loudly spits before he chugs the last of his beer and manages to drench his yellow polyester football shirt, and the helmet with a lightning bolt largely imprinted on the front side reeks of a good time. His can becomes lighter and hollow, so he gestures to the ice chest that sits next to the thirsty band. *This is my chance to escape*, I think to myself. I race to open up the top, dip my hand into frosty cubes, searching for the last beer at the bottom of the ice chest. Wiping the moisture from my arm on my jeans, I crack open the lid, so it is ready to be put to worthy use. Before making my way back, Tio Rick stops me while still playing his instrument.

"You see that lady over there?" He nods in her direction. "Her nickname is Fatter Than Me." "Why?" I dare to ask.

"Because she's fatter than me. I gave her that name in high school." He chuckles as his stomach bounces from side to side. "Didn't you see her cow tits and Jell-O ass? She looks like a fucken rhinoceros walking upright. Her face looks like one of those plastic masks you buy at Halloween time where the person is already dead," he adds as if 'Fatter Than Me' wasn't obvious enough to decipher. Tio Rick continues, "And that one, her name is Thunder Buns. Want to know why?"

"Because she has a tight ass," I answer the rhetorical question, shrugging my shoulders, "what does her face look like?" "Her face doesn't matter," Tio Rick snorts before turning into the microphone to continue his background singing.

"Not bad manners, just good beer," my dad belches out a booming burp, the drift knocking me back a few steps. We exchange containers so that he may continue his drinking marathon, and I am released to go play with my *primos*.

I sprint to the side of the red house, to a bundle of cousins that stand beside a trampoline crafted of canvas, whose springs are aged and others are missing. Cousin Cat pulls out a pack of crumpled line paper from the pocket of her Dickies overalls. "These are all numbered

1 through 10. Whoever draws the lowest number is it. Since I am the oldest, I get to pick my number first. And then Monchi and then Gabby, Esmi, and you get the idea." Nando kicks the dirt with his Pro Wing shoes that were previously owned by his two older brothers, the soles undone at the front, and his battered socks with holes loosely bend at his ankles. His legs are skeleton-like, with scabs that he picked so much the wounds have now become permanent on his skin. Everyone snatches a paper, and Nando is handed the last scrap. "Okay, Okay, open to see your number," Cat reminds us. I scramble to see mine, five. "Who's gonna be it?"

"Not me."

"I'm safe."

Cousin Ricky inhales and blows a puff of clear air. His round stomach matches his tubby knees. His charcoal skin is a similar shade to his father's. He staggers to the side of the trampoline, leans over it, and covers his eyes with his arm. The count begins, and we fling apart in various directions. Cat rushes to the junkyard area that contains inoperative clunkers withering annually, while Gabby dashes and ducks behind the peppertree with a junkyard tire, but I have a secret spot where I always hide. The front porch has a small opening on the side of the steps, so it's easy to bypass the gap, especially since it is covered with lofty, dehydrated grass. I cram through the tiny hole. As I creep through and make my way underneath the stairs, I glance to see Nando in the open area. His eyes remain wandering and lost. "Spizz," I buzz gently enough so he hears. He rotates, and I whisper again so that our eyes can meet. "Down here," I repeat. He smiles, his nose flattens, exposing the large gap between his two snaggleteeth. I reach through the waterless lawn, and he grips my hand as I tug him inside. We giggle silently and cover our mouths when footsteps approach. We recognize Ricky's pudgy leg stop as we become rigid.

"I see you," he wheezes tiredly between each word. His footprints kick up dirt, stumbling around the corner, where he notices his sister behind the peppertree. Nando crawls out the crack, and he drags me out, lifting me as much as his petite frame allows. Our hands together as one, we peek over the side of the red house to speculate. In the distance, the other cousins are already flying on the trampoline, having

3

reached safety. Cat's hair soars loosely in the sky, and Monchi blows on his cotton candy flavored bubble gum. I twist around to spot Ricky, who pierces oxygen through his nostrils, tiptoeing our way. I surge for the straightaway, and Nando's hands depart immediately from mine, before he climbs the stairs that lead inside the red house, each stride skipping a step, while Ricky follows the same pattern of footsteps. I make it to the trampoline untouched, even though my shoelaces came untied in the battle to protection. I gulp and bend over, putting my hands on my knees before I squat to fasten my LA Gears tighter. Quickly, I lift myself up and jog to the back door, waiting for Nando so that I can guide him to safety.

The adults are noisier and drunker than before, and I wander into the middle of the action. My grandpa sits on a cement block, blows on a *puro,* and turns to Tio Rick to give fatherly advice, *"Mijo, no te juntas con estas pinchis bolas de putas,"* referring to the skanks with funny nicknames. Cousin Imelda and my dad dance the "Bump." Imelda, with a different cigarette in her mouth, lifts her skirt and flashes her relatives. My dad, not to be outdone by the indecent exposure, rips off his shirt and rapidly twirls the torn cloth in the air, like a helicopter's propellers. He spins in a circle and awkwardly lands the half splits, one leg stretching to the front and the other tucks under his boney ass.

Coming from the back door, Nando staggers sluggishly, and Ricky walks closely besides him, holding his cousin's balance. Blood drains from Nando's head, and the gushing fluid spreads to his shirt. "He's bleeding!" a voice from the party circle yells. Nando, who was calm at the time, touches the deep cut and feels the dampness, and he closes his eyes before letting out a silent, then hysterical cry. The mob of grownups, with mouths reeking of tequila and Mexican beans, hurdle towards him.

"Get Chunky!" Cousin Imelda demands, her voice scratching against her throat. Part of her miniskirt folds inside her ass crack.

"He left. Got up in the middle of the party. Something about *her* being pissed about the partying, drinking, his shit talking brothers, the fun women, and the good time."

"Please," my dad sarcastically replies. "What does *she* want us to do? Play Patti Cakes and sing Kumbaya all day? We're no fuddy duddies. We are the best of the sorry bunch," my dad brags.

Tio Rick, who just finished packing the instruments, snatches Nando, lifting him off the ground, as Katie, Tio Rick's girlfriend, rushes inside the house. Tio Rick staggers to his truck and tosses Nando on the seat. Katie runs out the door, with a damp cloth in her hand, and makes her way to the vehicle. When she jumps in, Katie places the cloth on the open wound. The light blue Chevy truck, gyrates its wheels, and speeds off to the ER.

"How the hell did this happen?" Aunt Virgie, who was preoccupied cooking and eating the food during the party, demands to know while stuffing a tortilla chip in her mouth, her shirt stained with salsa and guacamole. My dad stands behind his sister and inflates his cheek with air, crossing his eyes, while Ricky tries to explain the situation without laughing.

"We were playing hide-in-seek. I chased Nando into the house, but he tripped over his shoe, and he fell. He hit his head on the edge of the doorway."

"Oh, for Christ's sake! That's why you don't run in the fucken house," Aunt Virgie scolds, jabbing a thick finger in her nephew's face. "This is why I don't have any damn kids!"

***

Many hours go by before Tio Rick calls from Mercy Hospital, and when he does, Aunt Virgie picks up the phone eagerly. I sit on the couch eavesdropping on the conversation between the two siblings. My dad snores on the carpet, his arm used as a pillow.

"His lopsided head could fit sixteen stiches?"

"You had to lie? About what?"

"And those fools at the hospital fell for it? I'm sure he could pass for your son, even though your skin is so dark— it's almost a nasty purple."

5

"You know, tough shit. This is as nice as I can get right now, considering the way the party ended, and I've been watching everyone else's turkey turd kids."

"I took them home."

"Yes, all five of them fit in my car. They only live a few miles away."

"They just walked in. The door was unlocked."

"I don't know. I didn't get off."

"I don't know if *she* was there nor do I give a rat's ass where *she* is."

"How the hell should I know? I've been calling since you left for the hospital. Their house phone keeps ringing."

"Everyone went home after that, except Ralph. He's passed out on the floor."

"He's your brother, too, you know."

"No, he's fine where he is. Let him take the trolley home in the morning."

"Because I'm the oldest of you, idiots, and I can make that decision."

"She's here, too. She's just looking at me."

"Your kids are asleep in the room."

"Well, hurry the hell up. Bill left when all this mess happened, and he's been waiting at home for me with our dog. I'm tired, I'm cranky, I'm hungry, and I want to leave."

Aunt Virgie slams the phone on the receiver. My dad tosses in his sleep and lets out a vulgar scream from within his dream. "Ralph, shut up!" Aunt Virgie takes off her *chancla*, doesn't aim, but hits her brother perfectly on his egg-shaped head. He doesn't waken, just rolls over on his back and breathes through his mouth. My dad, who drinks like a Mexican, wins a dance contest with his cousin, annoys his sister, and sprains his ankle while demonstrating his gymnastic moves, dozes on the ground. My dad, who is resting at my feet, but I never have to question how come he's not around.

Dear Veer!

Hey cuz'n. How's it going? Thank you for the letter and pictures. I was surprised to receive both from you. I'm okay I guess, just waiting to get off lockdown. That way, I can go to the yard. The other night I saw some guy get fucked up. It was like watching an ultimate fighting championship match live. Pretty exciting stuff. The "Woods" (white boys) had a little scuffle in my building with the "others." It was funny to me. I was faded off some jailhouse drink and had a view of everything. The highlight was when this one guy kicked a white boy in the face twice and knocked him out. Some real good action stuff you can't stage. Then, about a month later, the "Bull Dogs" (They're central California Mexicans) got into a riot with the "Northerners" (up North Mexicans). That was all bad for the "Northerners" because they were outnumbered fifty to twenty-three, but eleven of the Northerners didn't even help. So the ones who did got demolished. This all happened at the yard and very quickly. I was thinking of getting my first tattoo in here, but I'm not sure yet. Who knows, I might come out with a whole bunch.

Sounds like your trip to Prima Imelda's was one for the record book. I wonder what excuse my dad gave my mom to let him go on the trip unchaperoned. Did he tell his Facundo Gonzalez story? Chunk has a lot of good, funny little stories to tell, and he brings them to life so well. It's like I can see it in the sky, being shown like a projector. He can always bring a smile to my face on my worst day. What a guy! Tio Rick is always joking around and making fun of people. I miss his jokes and sarcasm. Then, when he's drunk, he always puts a little extra on it. There's never really any dull moment with him when he drinks. You know Virgie always has to eat at any little gathering. She's like the girl version of Chunk. They are twins. No matter how much she tried, she can't escape the fact that she's a Sanchez, just like all of us.

When I get out, maybe we can have a little something for me. But I would like it to be a surprise type thing. Not a surprise for me, but a surprise for everyone else. You know, have everyone there having a good time. Then, all of a sudden, I pop up. Until then, another day down, 1400 plus more to go.

A School Lesson

Every time it rains, the teachers in the after school program at Burbank force the bussed in students from Logan Heights to play inside, even though we would rather be outside competing in wall ball or co-ed kickball. After six hours of school, the inner city kids are transported from the beach back to their neighborhoods, waiting to release their pent-up energy from spelling words and written math problems.

A variety of board games tumble out of the cabinet as I search for the Connect Four, the box deteriorating at the edges. I settle myself on the dense carpet that spreads itself throughout the room; the cherry red schoolhouses and buttery yellow buses imprinted randomly on the rug. I set up the game, connecting the blue sides to the main piece so that it holds up. The checkers are an array on the floor. Anahi, who is seated alone in the corner, watches out the window with her chin resting on her palm as the rain pours thick on the bungalow ceiling. I nod my head at her, inviting her to come play, since I need a partner. She runs, accidently tripping over an intense Guess Who competition, and she perches in front of me, her legs crossed Indian style. Her shirt floats at the collar and sleeves. I prefer the black checkers because it is my favorite color, even though my teacher tells me black is not tehnically a color.

Soggy-shoe footsteps plod up the ramp. A hooded little boy, whose sleeves are too long and arms too short, tracks to the open door. Unexpectedly, Nando removes the covering, and I jump from the floor, crushing the pieces to the game. We throw ourselves in each other's arms, and I lift him from the ground, his feet dangling in the air as we choke in each other's bear hugs, my clothes now moist. Uncle Chunky gradually trots behind him.

"Big V, the Chunkster is here for you."

"Where's my dad?" I inquire still holding on to Nando.

9

"You're not happy to see Big Daddy?" My uncle, who has short legs and wide shoulders, winks at me as he wipes the water from his waxed handlebar mustache.

"It's Wednesday. It's his turn to pick me up." I remind him, placing Nando back on the ground.

"You're busting my chops, Big V. Your dad called me when I was leaving work. He wants me to take you to dance class. He will be there getting class started." I grab my backpack from the shelf and proceed outside. Nando follows me, and we skip singing, "Rain, rain go away. Please come back another day." We lift up our voices in a squeaky duet all the way to Uncle Chunky's truck, Black Beauty. When I get inside, I shake my head to rinse out the water. My shirt is soaked from the rain, so I roll up the bottom, twisting out the water, while goose bumps climb up my skin and through the hairs of my arms.

"Let's share my sweater," Nando kindly suggests. He lifts up his hoodie, and I jam my head underneath, squeezing one arm in the sleeve.

Uncle Chunky gets in, and the truck tilts to the left. His stomach touches the steering wheel. "How was your day at school?"

"It was fine I guess. I have spelling words to practice for my test on Friday. The words are easy: dazzle, riddle, cabbage, kettle."

"I'm sure you will ace it. You always liked to read."

"I ace all my tests. Ms. Sherman gives us ice cream if we get 100 percent."

"Are you scared of Ms. Sherman?" Uncle Chunky ponders.

"Of course not," I express with amusement.

"Why should she be, Chunk?" Nando already referring to his dad on a first name basis.

"I remember my teachers were scary looking." Uncle Chunky starts his engine and pulls out into the street as the bottom of the truck momentarily scraps the road. "What do your teacher's call you?"

"By her name, Chunk." Nando replies for me.

"Yeah, by my name, Vera." I add.

"Do they call you by your full name, Veracruz? And you, by your full name, Fernando?"

A bit embarrassed, I answer first, "No. It's cut in half, but I'm glad. My name is too long, too many letters, too Mexican. I'm not too thrilled that my name is a compound word, like bathroom or homework."

"Yeah, Chunk. Three syllables each name and eight letters a piece? You have to admit, that's long for any culture."

"That happened to me in school. My name changed from Ramon to Raymond. In school, our names were Americanized by our teachers." The windshield wipers scoop the rain as Uncle Chunky heads past the stop sign. "Then, there was a new kid in school named Facundo Gonzalez, from Sinaloa. When he showed up to school, the principal announced an emergency administrative meeting. I snuck up to the door and heard them discussing the possibilities of changing his name. The teachers wanted to shorten his name to F-A-C, Fac. But that didn't sound right. It sounded like the bad word. 'Where's Fac? Have you seen Fac today? Fac, where's your homework? Fac, you have detention.' They couldn't shorten his name, and they were freaking out. He was the only kid in school to keep his full name."

***

As we pull up to the front parking lot of the Boys and Girls Club, I unwrap myself from Nando's sweater.

"Here you go, Big V. Tell your dad to stop calling me at four in the morning."

"I will, but he probably won't listen. Can Nando come to dance class with me? After all, his brothers and sisters are folklorico dancers too."

"He needs to come with me. There is an event going on at Jack Murphy Stadium. We need to collect the cans in the parking lot and cash them in at the recycling place on Federal Ave."

"In the rain?" I cross-examine as I place my backpack over my head.

"We have our *panchos* underneath the seat. He'll be joining you one day. Hurry inside. You're getting wet."

"Okay, but promise me that one day you will be my dance partner," I request of Nando.

"I promise. Bye, Veracruz." Nando says as he glows from ear to ear with the satisfaction of knowing that I dislike my full name.

"*Adios*, Fernando. Thank you, Ramon." I return the birth names.

I slam the door and run to the entrance of the recreation room, turning around just as Uncle Chunky drives off. Nando ecstatically gazes my way and waves goodbye, as his long lips smile and shine through the muddy day.

I hope you had a happy Thanksgiving. By the sounds of it, I know you did. As for me, it was okay, I guess. They gave us white rice smothered with some type of light orange sauce with chicken in it. Sides included mixed veggies, two pieces of wheat bread with a little buttercup, black eye peas, and a brownie for dessert. I washed it all down with Kool-Aid. It didn't fill me up, but I am content for now. If I get hungry later, I will likely drink a lot of water from the fountain. Plus, I don't celebrate holidays while I'm in places like these. I don't really like the way Thanksgiving came about or why we are supposed to celebrate. I only liked it when I was little because we didn't have to go to school.

It pleases me to know that you enjoy my letters for I also enjoy yours. They are always exciting and full of gossip of our crazy familia. I really like to read about your wild adventures. When I get out, we can go on some of our own, together, just like when we were kids, always up to no good.

I remember when I would go joy riding with Cat and Noe in his Prelude before they had Monnie. One time, they let me shoot a BB gun out of the window when we were driving down Imperial Ave. I used to have little frog legs when I was younger, and sometimes, they called me Kermit. Now, everyone has their own little families except you and I, even though I've had three different girls pregnant before. I somehow managed not to have a little nigglet running around. One of them had two abortions and one miscarriage. I didn't make her get them. She chose to, just for the record. I almost had some girl pregnant when I was sixteen, but luckily, her period ended up coming, almost three weeks late. Boy, that sure was a scary moment. All the other times I was an adult. The most recent was before I got locked up. She got an abortion on her own without me having a say in the matter. No one knows but you.

I can't wait to get out and drink with the family. I don't like beer. It doesn't taste good to me. I'm gonna have a bottle of cognac with my dad at the house, while my sisters cook some good grub. That will be my welcome home gift to myself. I know from now on, though, I'm going to cherish every family gathering we have because I done missed too many. Gonna miss more, and ain't no telling how many I'll have when I get out with all the ones I love or if the ones I love will even be there for me to hug when I do touch back down.

Simple Words

Once, my dad thought someone was calling him a name. "I'm not a moron."

"No, I'm not calling you a moron. I said oxymoron. Your sentence had an oxymoron in it."

He turned to me. "What's an oxymoron?" Ralph asked me to elaborate.

"It's like you advising someone to behave," was my impertinent remark.

***

Ralph hands over a wrinkled dollar that I must split with my brother for the ice cream truck. "Behave," he forewarns as he donates the currency. "And tell your uncle to hurry up." I place the dollar in my back pocket, and we exit the car, walking towards Uncle Chunky's house, the rooftop cluttered with old tennis shoes, a bike handle, a soccer ball with no air, and a broken chair with no legs. A dream catcher is pinned to the archway of the porch, and it lightly swings in the dust of the summertime.

"What's the word on the street, Big V?" Uncle Chunky asks, as he strolls out of the house, making his way to my dad's car.

"The streets want to know when your truck will get fixed?"

"I don't know. The engine blew out. I'm going to ask Hitler for a loan."

"Who's Hitler?"

"My boss."

"Why do you call your boss Hitler?"

"Because she has the same mustache as him, I think. I really don't know. I didn't give her that name."

"Who gave it to her?"

"Rick. Who else?"

"What other nicknames does he have for people?"

"Oh boy, oh boy. Well, there's Moon Head, Walnut Face, Bubble Eyes, The Bride of Frankenstein, Raunchy Ruby, Chocolate, Skitzo, his wife, Skitza."

"Vera, go inside the house. We're both going to be late for work if you keep asking questions." My dad interupts.

For various summer days, Cousin Cat babysits us, since my dad works the nine to five at the M.A.C. Project. She stands at the door, waves at my dad, making her presence known, and immediately returns into the house, grabbing the telephone, where her homegirl is waiting to chat about the cute boys in Mr. Hartunian's Algebra class. I peek inside the house as my brother impatiently runs inside to join Wicho, who is glued to the Nintendo system and aiming an orange plastic gun at the television, massacring flying ducks one by one.

I park myself on the porch and watch as the neighbor's chickens disperse loosely in the front yard. Cars slow down and point to the livestock, which I'm sure makes for a striking conversation. The other neighbors, to the left of the house, are gone for the day, and I contemplate on sneaking into their driveway to play basketball since they have the only hoop on the block. Besides, my dad said I couldn't leave the house to go to the rec center and play ball with boys twice my age. A collection of athletic equipment had already tumbled from the roof of Uncle Chunky's house. I pick up the basketball and dribble a few times to make sure there is enough air inside.

On my way to the neighbors, I pause, hearing the chimes of the ice cream truck increase in the distance. I trail out of the yard, briefly chasing the mobile frozen dessert store, my shoes flowing on the gravel street and the basketball bouncing to the speed of my footsteps. The man, dressed in an apron and a cutoff t-shirt, comes to a stop as he notices the herd in the rear view mirror. A batch of neighborhood children crowd around to slobber on funky ice cream bars shaped to resemble trendy images of the year: Barbie, He-Man, Jem, and Batman. The scrawny lad in front of me orders a drumstick, Lucas candy, *saladitos*, and a Mexican toy. He hands the driver ten quarters, places the items in his pocket, and hurries out of the way as two kids, who are a foot shorter, chase after him. When my time arrives, I pull out the crinkled bill and give it to the *paletero*, who hands me a bigstick that isn't as fancy as the popular cartoon characters, who have bubble gum for eyes, but is just as mouthwatering.

I return to my uncle's front yard, working on my crossover and eating skills at the same time. I devour my ice cream while observing the tots that pass by or play in the streets. Some jump rope on the corner while others wet one another with water hoses in order to cool off from the summer heat. Teens, with their walkmans and seasonal shades, stroll to the trolley station so that they can chill at the Lemon Grove mall.

Knocking the basketball out of my hand, Nando forcefully passes in front of me. He jumps in Black Beauty, which is parked in the driveway, and locks himself inside with the windows rolled up. The tires need air, the back glass cracked from being hit by tiny rocks, as the boiling rays of the sun peek through the glass. His Ninja Turtle t-shirt has a rip on the threads of the armpits, and his shorts are covered with dirt. Nando's head is down and his chest heaves from his panting. As he slightly looks up, his swollen eyes make him look tired and scared. I observe his body language and wander over to the driver's side, flicking my popsicle stick on the grass. I tap on the window to get his attention, but he doesn't budge. I tap again. "Nando, let me in." He slowly glares into my eyes, and my countenance becomes stiff and worried. "I'll buy you an ice cream," I bribe, pressing my last three quarters against the window. Nando slowly unlocks the door and scoots over. I climb in beside him, slamming the decayed door with both my arms. "What's wrong?" I ask in a low tone, placing the quarters in his palm. His sobs grow louder and his breathe shorter.

Nando waits awhile before he answers with a heartbreaking sound, "Nobody loves me." I close my eyes for a few seconds, as tears begin to form, before I open them again. My emotions darken because of my cousin's pain.

"I love you," I respond, while shifting him closer to me. Nando sinks himself into my shoulder, and I cradle his head, hugging him, so he'll forgets the words, and together, we cry.

You are very welcome, but you don't have to thank me. I'm just being me and a good cousin to you. After all, that's what family is supposed to be for, ain't it? To talk to each other and try to lift one another up when they're down. If all of us did that, a lot of things would be easier or better than they are. I've been a little down too, lately, but I've also tried not to let it get to me because if I do, I'm just gonna end up making things worse. I can only hold so much in or hold so much back until it starts to overflow and pour out. I've been doing a lot of the same stuff you're doing, and it seems like no matter how hard we try, we never seem to see any good results. Or when we do get some good results, some other bullshit will happen to make that go away and put us further back.

Now, about your little prediction, it sounds a bit logical but also outrageous. I just want you to look after me if you do go, you know like my guardian angel, and I will be yours, too, if I go first. I have pondered about death plenty of times. One time, when I was younger, even before my teens, I had grabbed a knife and ran up to the top of our hill and sat in the moonlight with it in hand, holding the sharp part against my wrist, contemplating death, while tears ran down my face.

A few other times, I wished I was dead, but changed my mind after deciding that there were too many other things in life that I wanted to do or have before I die. Then, I started having déjà vu. I would have a weird dream, not knowing what it means, then, out of nowhere, my dream would come true, taking place in real life. My first one took place at camp when I first got locked up, which makes me a bit worried because when I was younger, I had dreams of being in prison and getting stuck—then, waking up in a hospital room with a whole bunch of tubes in me. I had a few of those. I also had dreams where I get shot up, and I lay on the concrete, leaking in the streetlights, waiting for an ambulance.

One time, I was at the old Lemon Grove bowling alley when some shooting occurred. I ran right in front of the guy with the gun, but luckily, I didn't get hit. Then, there were times when I was out, there were some close calls. I left my homie's spot where we were kicking it at the store real quick and, a minute after I left, someone came through and started shooting. My homie I was with earlier got hit in his leg. He lived, and, luckily, I wasn't there.

But life is crazy like that, I guess. Some things are meant, and some things aren't meant to be. All I know is that we only have one life to live, so make it count, and your future is in your hands, so try not to drop it because if you do, it's gonna be hard trying to pick up the pieces of your life and putting them back together. I'm so far behind; it's all bad. Someday, I will catch up, though. Just got to stay more focused on the important things and not get lost in the bullshit. Don't even really know if there's a heaven or hell. Sometimes, I don't even care. I just hope that all my loved ones will make it to a better place. Some say heaven is in the sky and hell is under the ground. Some say heaven is what you make of it, and hell is what you go through to get there. I say, we all got to die someday, and that day is when we find out the truth for ourselves.

A Daunting Motion Picture

Cat is one of those babysitters who let us do whatever we want and watch whatever we want. If it was my choice, I wouldn't pick a scary movie. The popcorn heats in the microwave, and Nando dispenses cups of soda for his siblings and cousins. "Coke for you and Sprite for you," he hands Wicho and Esmi their thirst-quenchers before he chooses a spot next to me on the floor. Since the winter tends to bring in the chilly gust, I tangle myself in a blanket, my hands poking out from a gap. I shift my bangs away from my face, so that I don't chew my hair in the process of sipping on my drink. Cat comes out from the kitchen and places a bowl in the center of the coffee table. "There's plenty for everyone, so don't make a mess. I have enough chores to do around the house," she reminds us. Without taking turns, we dig our hands in the container, getting more popcorn on the floor than in our mouths.

"Esmi is making a mess, like she always does." Wicho points her way.

"No, I'm not, punk," Esmi quickly picks up the corn and places them in her mouth.

Wicho grabs a handful and throws it in her face. Esmi doesn't back down from her brother, and kicks him in his knee.

"Okay whoever doesn't shut up, I will wrestle them to the ground," Monchi, his hair slicked back and styled with gel, demonstrates a double leg take down with the air. Cat turns off the lights and puts the video in the VHS.

"By the way, this is a true story, so believe everything you see." Cat announces. My eyes circle the room to observe the reactions of my cousins. I'm the only one who seems scared.

"Do you think that is true?" My brother whispers in my ear so no one else hears him.

"I hope not." I softly reply.

"Don't be such a scaredy cat. It's not like the monster is going to jump out the screen and bite you." Esmi butts into the conversation.

"Esmi is not being quiet." Wicho tells again on his sister.

Monchi, keeping to his promise, clutches her in a headlock, "Are you going to shut up now?" He squeezes her a little harder but just enough for her to murmur her words.

"Yes, yes. I promise I won't say anything else." Monchi releases her, and Esmi glares her brothers.

As the movie begins, the words flash in large thick red letters, "The Exorcist." Creepy low chanting and light piano playing begin in the introductory credits, causing me to believe there is a ghost in the room. I hug myself, trying to compose my fear so that it is not obvious, secretly doing the sign of the cross underneath my blanket. The possessed little girl, with scabs and puss that ooze from her face, spins her head and vomits a lime green liquid. "Fuck you, mother fucker!" Her smoky voice, like a demon, laughs at the priest, claims she is the devil. I cringe at how she floats in the air, stabs herself underneath, foaming blood from her mouth, her white eyes roll to the back of her head. Her dark room filled with fog, cold enough to see one's breath, a rattling bed, flickering candles, shadows on the Virgin Mary, doors closing on their own, the power of Christ, holy water that burns. The girl, now, strapped to the bed, "in time, in time," she repeats, scripture on her stomach, carved by an invisible knife, may the Lord be with you, let us pray.

I don't care what name Esmi calls me at this point. I jerk from the television and leap from the floor, racing out of the living room haunted by thoughts of demons and moving furniture. I run into Cat's room, covering my ears and closing my eyes. I feel a hand tugging at the blanket, uncovering my ears, even though I am planning to stay in this position until everything is over. I open my eyes one at a time, and Nando is standing right in front of me. He knows I am frightened, unwilling to return to the eerie living room. He understands.

"I'm not going back. They can make fun of me all they want."

"You'll be alright, cousin."

"No, I won't. I'm going to have nightmares again."

"It's okay to have nightmares. We all have them."

"But I'm scared."

Nando embraces his arms around mine, "No need to be. I'm with you. I'll keep you safe, like you do to me when I get sad and lonely."

"You will?"
"I cross my heart. I will be your guardian angel, forever."

I've been okay for the most part, just trying to work my program as smoothly as I can. But this is still prison, so anything can happen. All I can do is stay out the way and keeping minding my own because that alleviates the majority of problems or altercations and scenarios that lend to fighting, violence, and bloodshed. I got to try to keep a level head and calm myself. That way, I can individually avoid these types of situation. There's already been a few close calls, so let us hope that there won't be anymore. So for now, I will just continue to take it one day at a time.

One of the things I look forward to here is the movies they put on. We have a movie channel and usually every Tuesday we watch new movies. I have seen I Am Legend, and this week, I'll see Transformers and National Treasure: Book of Secrets. No rated R's, though.

Painting is fun. I used to draw people's tattoo patterns. I used to enjoy it whenever we did it in school. I don't remember what I did with my paintings, though. Maybe I'll give it a little go again when I get out and get situated. Maybe we can do a nice amount of paintings, together, and we can try to sell them on EBay or at Chicano Park.

We have books in here. We got a library, too. I know a lot of people use if for legal stuff. I like Harry Potter. I was planning on watching all of them in a row when I get out. I already read all the books, so I know how it turns out. They are all pretty damn good, if you ask me. Very well written. I plan on reading the dictionary and try to expand my vocabulary. I've been playing Scrabble, too. It's really fun and educational. Me and this other guy go at it, but sometimes we play three or four ways.

You can send me books, but make sure they are paperbacks. You can send me magazines, too. I like "Show" and "Curves." As for books, suspense is good and anything educational. The books I mostly read since I've been here are urban books because that's what's in the yard the most. Fiction is cool, too, so whatever you think is good, send it. I am sure your book will be great also. Maybe we can find a success story to put in about myself, but we'll just have to wait to see what the future holds. Maybe one day, I might be able to inspire.

Mexican Meals

When my dad first moved into the apartments in National City, I expressed to him it was the best place ever because it had a pool and a nearby 7-11 with a Pac-Man arcade game. Uncle Chunky leaves his kids with Ralph during the summer. My dad earned a different position as an elementary counselor, so he has some months off, which makes him the certified built-in babysitter, to use the term loosely. I'm not sure if my dad watching children is a good or bad thing, even if the services are free, considering he slugged a P.E. teacher, told a priest to go to hell, and once blew up a car by pouring river water down the engine hole.

My dad departs to the laundry room across the complex before the *bola* arrives. I flip the channel to the Tiny Tunes cartoons, but my stomach craves some loving, since I haven't eaten breakfast yet.

I trek to the kitchen and open the fridge, catching a draft of the chilly breeze. Tio Rick would bring premade sandwiches and chips by the crates he got for *gratis* from the park and rec after school program, splitting the food between his brothers' household without the approval of his boss, Mr. Potato Head. Since I had grown worn out of eating the premade sandwiches, I reach for a typical Mexican meal, a *tortilla* with butter. I turn the knob to the stove and lay the *tortilla* on the rack. I am hesitant to flip the *tortilla* over, so it catches on fire. The flames spread through the flour and begin to crack.

Over at the red house, the same situation transpired. I had chucked the flaring *harina* in the trashcan and left. My dad blasted in and riotously panicked. He put out the flames with water, and when grilled, I blamed it on nana's cat, Tiger.

Now, there is no cat to blame. Nando enters the apartment. He walks in with a bow and arrow in hand. The bowstring is made of his father's elastic underwear band, the kind with blue and yellow stripes, the whitey tighties. Nando drops his homemade arrow bow and laughs at my error. He coolly turns off the burner, and the flames, on the *tortilla*, die down. My heartbeat gradually becomes regular, as Nando rescues me from trouble.

"Hurry, throw that away before my dad comes back."

"We can't have any evidence!"

"Should I take out the trash?"

"No, that looks too obvious. Like you're trying to hide something. The trashcan isn't even full."

"Ooh. What are you doing?" TJ comes from outside our room, his WWF action figure in hand.

"Don't worry about what we are doing. Just get your ass back inside that room, and mind your own business or else I'll let dad know about the girly magazine underneath your bed," I demand.

"Whatever. I hope dad finds out." He shuts the door to continue his Royal Rumble fantasy.

"What if he finds the tortilla? He'll know I burnt it and had the stove on without permission."

"I'll put it at the very bottom, so he doesn't see it." Nando pushes over an old corndog box, crumbled napkins, a filter filled with roasted coffee, orange pilings, and an empty liter of milk.

"Okay. You're right." I give Nando a relieved grin. "How do you know about this evidence stuff?"

"I watch a lot of cop shows. That's what I want to be when I grow up, you know, a cop, someone who saves people."

We return to watching the television, and we don't mention the *tortilla* anymore. As I glance out the open door, I see my dad, with the laundry basket on the hood of Uncle Chunky's truck, gossiping in his brother's ear.

"Ray, what do you have to *say* on this Fri*day*." Ralph tries to rhyme by exaggerating the ending word. "I wrote a poem this morning about you, since you don't like it when I call you at five a.m.."

"I'm not here to listen to poetry. I'm swing by to drop off Nando."

"Hah! You can't swing anywhere so just listen. I have a big brother named, Chunk. In high school, he was a hunk. Then, he met *her*, and *she* called him a skunk. But that's ok because he's still my big brother, Chunk."

"Is that it?"

"It's a haiku, short, sweet and to the point."

"That was like listening to fucken Shakespeare."

"Wait until you hear the one I wrote about your *her*."

"*She's* still upset because *she* walked through your cloud of farts. You do that on purpose every time you see *her*. Your farts smell like a fucken sewer."

"Then, *she* should stay away, right. If *she* gets close to me again, I'll throw holy water in *her* face, so *she* melts."

"Jive sucker."

Nando and I listen to our dads' smearing conversation from the door. We share our jokes too, but ours will remain private.

How about those Chargers! We beat up on Houston real good. Now, it is time to do the same to the Vikings. Then, after the Colts beat the Patriots to make them have a loss, we gonna beat the Colts to keep them from going undefeated. I didn't get to see the Monday Night game either, but I listened to it. People in my dorm kept looking at me funny because I was yelling and cussing loudly. We pulled it off, though, and I won some soups. Should be another good game this Sunday. Now, we just got to keep rolling for the next three games and all the way through the playoffs. Our defense needs to step up a bit more, along with the running game. Our team needs to be complete and balanced because that's when we are at our best, when we are the most dangerous. There's nothing like a tailgate at the Charger game with the family. I sure do miss those dog piles. I remember sometimes I would be scared to get caught on the bottom of them. Now, I just hope I can enjoy another one with everyone, just like back in the day, and it wouldn't matter if I'm on the bottom because I can take it now.

So where is The Office located at? It's hard not to have a good time when my dad and Tio Rick are playing. They know how to liven up a party and get everyone going. You know, as well as I do, that all that partying all night and drinking has its repercussions the next day. But, we don't care because it's well worth it. That would have been a funny thing to watch—you, Ralph, and my dad disco dancing. I can't believe my dad had to drive Virgie home. Wow, even your brother showed up. I don't think he likes being around the family because of the way we act. I used to be like that. I would rather be running in the streets getting into something I shouldn't be getting into.

You know, it ain't a good time if someone doesn't take a good spill. I'm sure it was a good time and the next will be the same, if not better. Hopefully, The Office will still be jumping when I get out, so we can check it out. What my brother getting some action? It must have been all the good looks that were passed down to us from Big Chunk. Just wait until the rucas get a load of me when I get out. Not only will I have the good looks, but I will have the body to go with it. Thanks for the flicks; they are greatly appreciated. My brothers look like they both put on some weight. Must be all that good eating. Tell your friend, Patty, that if she doesn't mind, I could use some counseling sessions. I have plenty of issues we can discuss.

But as for my dad, I was unaware of his situation. Last time I called, he was there and seemed okay; no one mentioned anything. It must have happened afterwards. He is always cheerful and keeping high spirits through these types of situations; that's him. I'm hoping everything will be fine. We cannot fear time because we cannot control it or stop it. We must live and deal with it and what it brings upon us. Whether it's good, bad, or ugly, we can't escape it. We have to decide for ourselves whether or not to face it, accept it, and deal with it.

A Super Bowl Party

Mexican people don't need a reason to throw a party, but when we do have one, we go all out. The Super Bowl starts in a few hours. Tio Rick custom designed a wooden lightning bolt to display in the front yard so that the cars driving down Jamacha Road can honk their horns and cheer as they cruise by. My cousins and I wave our blue and gold, miniature pompoms to show our football spirit before kickoff. A keg of Miller Lite stands in a tub already tapped and chilled with ice. Carne and pollo asada fizzle on the grill with beans and rice steaming on the oven top as diced onions, chopped cilantro, and sliced tomatoes wait, ready to decorate an appetizing street style taco.

In order to be the #1 Charger fan for the day, Cousin Ricky insist on shaving a lightning bolt in the back of his head. I am my dad's hairstylist and convince Ricky I can perform the job, like the way they do at old school barbershops that have checker floors and framed black and white photos pinned on the wall. I walk to the bathroom, which smells of Old Spice cologne and Irish Spring bar soap, grabbing a hand towel and the clippers from underneath the sink. As I walk back, Ricky calmly waits, in a fold up chair in the middle of the kitchen floor. I place the towel around his neck so the little hairs won't scratch his skin. I blow dust off the grooming equipment before plugging the cord into the socket.

"Do you want me to get a radio and play old school music so you feel like you're at a real barbershop?" I try to persuade so Ricky feels more confident in my hairstyling techniques.

"Naw, just do your business." He persists as I lightly push his head forward.

"What the hell are you doing?" TJ enquires coming in from the back door. The clippers are already buzzing, and I start to carve zig-zags.

"I'm going to shave a lighting bolt in the back of his head." I explain as a pile of Ricky's hair begins to form on the ground.

"You're going to mess it up, like you do everything else!" My brother suggests that I will not perform at a proficient level.

29

"I know what I'm doing. I cut Ralph's hair all the time—"

"Dad's head is easy. All you do is shave the two lumpy horns growing from the back." TJ interrupts.

"It's not your head, so don't worry about it." I don't look his way, just continue my craftwork.

Nando and Wicho walk in during the process of my entrepreneur skills. They come close to see the mess I created on Ricky's skull. The bottom portion of our cousin's hair is gone, while the top half remains thick and black.

"What is that supposed to be? It looks all jacked up." Nando laughs, the scar he acquired from the red house shining on his bald head. His SD Charger shirt shows the faces of Junior Seau, Leslie O'Neal, Natrone Means, and Stan Humphries in cartoon form, big heads and little bodies.

"It's a Charger bolt," I explain proudly.

"I told you it wasn't going to look good," TJ reminds me.

"His hair looks like Moe from the Three Stooges. Shank!" Nando gently socks his cousin on the side of his stomach.

"I want to see it. Give me a mirror." Ricky demands, removing the towel from his neck as he stands up.

"There is no mirror. You'll just have to see it later." I say, sweeping the hairs from the ground and dumping them in the trashcan.

Kickoff begins. Nando and I lounge next to each other at the corner of the couch, while Wicho and TJ proceed to laugh at Ricky's awful mop. We fly up off behinds, almost knocking over the generic name brand sodas that are by our feet, as the Chargers get equipped on defense. My dad chants to get us excited for the opening play, "L-S-D! Everyone L-S-D!" He shapes his arms into the letters. "Again, L-S-D," his "S" looking like an Egyptian dance. "Look, Sharp, Defense! L-S-D! Yaay!" Ralph amusingly applauds and gives himself a standing ovation.

"Ralph, sit your ass down. The rest of us are trying to watch the damn game," Aunt Virgie yells. "My dog behaves better than you." As proof, Cocoa calmly lies on the carpet floor, with her eyes closed.

Sitting down and sarcastically crossing his legs, Ralph responds, "Don't you need to feed Cocoa? She looks hungry. Go in the kitchen, and don't return until the game is over," he waves his arms to shoo Aunt Virgie away, like a fly.

"She already ate." Aunt Virgie rolls her eyes and mixes her plate of beans with rice.

"Feed her again."

"No, idiot, dogs only eat once a day."

"Then, how come you don't take your own advice? Kids, make sure you eat your fruits and vegetables so you don't end up looking like your aunt."

"Ralph, make sure you don't shit in your fucken pants again, like you did at the Padres game. You're lucky they were giving out free towels that day, and you were able to wrap it around your waist, so nobody saw your brown shit stains. You need to start wearing fucken diapers."

My dad turns to Nando and me, "Who do you think would win in a race, me or your favorite fat aunt?"

"Asshole."

"Hello? Football is on TV. The Chargers are in the Super Bowl for the first time, in case you forgot. *Chingado*," Tio Rick points the remote at the screen and blasts the volume so that his kin shut up.

"And the San Diego Chargers are on the board with their first touchdown of the game," the broadcaster reports to the viewers. Nando jumps on top of Wicho in an attempt to drag him to the ground. The rest of us create a tower of bodies, crushing him to the ground, knocking over our sodas.

"You morons are making a mess!" Aunt Virgie scolds, as we continue to jam our bodies together.

"Okay, my ribs hurt. Get off me." Tio Rick, who sometimes forgets his age, rolls over on his stomach, "Help me up, fuckers. I'm stuck."

We slowly peel off one another, and it takes the strength of all the cousins to get Tio Rick off the floor.

"In another spectacular play, Steven Young connects to Jerry Rice in the end zone for a third touchdown pass," the NFL announcer delivers a recap of the play.

"I have another chant. V-L-C!" This time, my dad yanks us from our seat. Nando and I join in and form the letters with our arms. I stand

31

behind him, looking over his head; Nando's palming his football while we arrange our limbs to become letters. "V-L-C! *Vete La Chingada*!" Ralph applies the cuss word to express his dislike of the 49er lead. The rest of the family joins in on the swearing as the game proceeds to the final quarter, and Aunt Virgie no longer cares if Ralph is in the way of the television.

By the time the game comes to a close, we already completed a football game of our own in the streets; the piñata in pieces; the candy eaten; the fourth batch of meat smoked on the grill; pictures taken in both day and night time; the jump-for-joy deflated; and more runs to the liquor store than timeouts during the game.

In the backyard under the Bolt canopy, Tio Rick and Uncle Chunky play their acoustic guitars, their instruments of pleasure. Uncle Chunky presses his *jarana* against his Charger wool *pancho*, "San Diego Super Chargers. San Diego Super Chargers. San Diego Super Chargers, Charge!"

Cat and Monchi legally drink their beer, while Gabby holds little Lucy, who claps to the beat of her grandpa's guitar.

"Thunder bolts and lighting gonna light up the sky. We got a plan. Gonna do it for a super fan." Tio Rick sings, harmonizing with his brother.

Ricky wears an adjustable Charger cap to cover up his new, creative hairstyle while TJ and Wicho toss the pigskin over Tata's head, who sits quietly, looks, and smokes.

My dad purposely falls to the ground. Nando and I spring over him, as he rolls back and forth on the ground, like a moving log in a river. Ralph reaches his arms in the air, and Nando and I lift him to his feet. He launches us on each of his side while we form the "whip." In a single file line, we sway as one, kicking anyone that gets in our path. My dad lets us go, and we catch each other, twirling together, the family enjoying the evening as if we were the Super Bowl champs.

It's true what they say, "You never truly know what you have until it's gone." Sometimes losing something really opens your eyes, though. It can be a trip sometimes to find out how you can relate to others around you, whether they are young or old. It's usually someone you wouldn't expect. I used to feel trapped, like when I was younger, and I would be home alone. Or even when I would be the only kid at the house. It happened often, at times. Pretty weird, considering I have three sisters and two brothers; just goes to show how much everyone liked being out of that house, away from everyone else. My dad is a good example 'till this day.

Sometimes, we might think what is best isn't, and sometimes, we might be confused all in one, while trying to gain happiness, only to make the wrong decision, causing us to lose sight of what happiness lies ahead. It is something so simple, sometimes we're even unable to notice or find it. Then, when we do notice, it is gone, just like that.

It's crazy that someone can be here one day and gone the next. There are very few things that are certain and death is one of them. You can't run or hide from it because if it wants you, it will get you. I'm sure things will get easier eventually and not just for you, but for me, too. We just got to keep hope alive no matter how hard things get or how depressing things may seem. We got to continue to power through the strife. We will most certainly die one day, but until that time comes, we must continue to live our lives, live our lives how we want to, live our life to the fullest, live our life hopeful and fearless. Even though at times, we may not be the wisest, we must always survive the nonsense, the craziness, the weariness, and the darkness. For we are not certain of what lies ahead, but no matter what it is, we must live through it and overcome it, in order to make it through life. Stay strong because I'm going to do the same

Like a Knife Coming at You

Mixed tapes are the greatest invention in the world. I can record my favorite singers all in one cassette Janet Jackson, MC Hammer, BBD, Madonna, and Paula Abdul. It's the latest trend to swap music with friends and family. Ricky inserts a mixed tape in his Walkman and places the earphones over his head, while Tio Rick, in his bedroom, listens to the phone messages for the day. I turn on the T.V. and play along with the survey questions on Family Feud.

"I bet you I can get most of the top answers." I explain to Ricky, who can't hear me.

"Who from the family should we take on the show if we ever went on the show? It would probably be a mess, pretty dysfunctional. Don't you think?" I continue talking to myself. "Everyone would argue before going on the show. We'd get kicked off, for sure."

Ricky's jaw begins to tense, and he hurries to take off the earphones, "Dad," he yells from the living room couch, "come listen to this!" Tio Rick, who was about to change, comes out with his guayabera shirt halfway button down.

"Dad!"

"Que hombre?"

"I was listening to a tape I borrowed from Wicho. Then, this came on." Ricky places the tape in the stereo system for us to hear and slowly presses play, appearing a bit nervous.

The music was interrupted. "None of you are allowed to speak unless I give you permission! None of you are allowed to eat unless I say you can eat! I can't even look at any of you because you all make me sick!" *Her* voice ugly and sharp, like a razor cutting into the skin. "You're already a fat pig! Look at yourself! You're a disgrace! A fat, disgusting disgrace to me!" The loud echo in *her* soul, violent and intimidating, *her* words bite like a deadly vapor, *her* words sound like stepping on broken glass. "I hate all of you!" The background silent and tense. "My heart hurts every day! I have pain because of all of you! It's all your fault! There is no God to rescue you!" *She* lets out a slight giggle before a hand slaps against an open cheek. *Her* heart black from hate, unworthy love. This is the ugliest noise I ever heard. "You are all dead to me! Nobody will ever love you! Nobody!" A squeaky voice pipes up, "Bitch, shut the fuck up!" His tone clear-cut and firm even though he is the youngest. *She* races into the room, footsteps recorded, and a door loud enough that swings open. "Did you tell me to shut the fuck up?" *She* dangerously roars, and the tape stops, running out of space.

We stare at each other. We're all mute, and no words can describe what I just heard. This was far more than verbal abuse because *she* meant it. *She* doesn't love. Nando, the youngest of all the siblings, had the courage to speak when others kept their mouths shut. That's just the kind of person he is. Even when the other person is bigger than him, Nando's bravery always stands stronger.

> *I kind of got used to the weather up here, so it doesn't bother me as much as it used to. I just don't like it when it's still in the 90's, and it's nighttime. It makes it hard to sleep. Supposedly, I fit the criteria for the "involuntary out of state transfer," so they say. Either way, it doesn't look so good for me. I'll keep you updated when I find out for sure what's going on.*

> *Can't wait to be around everyone again and enjoy their company. I have to remember to check out Tia Virgie's photos albums when I get out so that I could see all the priceless flicks she has of the family. Damn, that sucks about Lucy. I was really hoping she wouldn't go down that road. But, I hate to say that there was always that one single thought in my mind that there was always a chance she might take up after her grandma's side of the family. I really hope she can get it together because I don't want to see her go out like that. I wish I was out just to try and help her feel better and not throw away her life and beauty. It's really sad thinking about her whole situation, pregnant at such a young age, and how she was brought up and driven to do the things she does and act the way*

36

she acts. I know she probably feels like no one loves her or cares about her. And the only way to make it better is to get away from those that cause physical and emotional pain and suffering.

It's crazy; I was thinking about how I saw Gabby at Mullins. It's a liquor store on 30th and Imperial, one of my hangout spots. Well, I was driving my brother's Cadillac. I had one of my little cha chas with me. Gabby was buying beer for her and Charles. She was looking sad and depressed. I ended up giving her a ride back home, and we talked a little. She broke down and started crying. I tried to comfort her the best I could, and I told her to just try her best to take care of the kids. As I was reminiscing on the night, I wish I would have checked in on them and made sure they at least had cereal, milk, and stuff to make sandwiches. Even more, I wish I would have had a talk with Lucy to let her know that she could call me if she ever needed anything because I know what it feels like to want to get away when it hurts. Plus, I tend to be in that area a lot because that's my gang turf. I was wishing I would have done that because I had a little bit of money at the time. Plus, they are my immediate family.

I know one time when I was downtown doing my thing and what not, I ran into Gabby and Lucy in front of Horton Plaza. She was taking Lucy to get some shoes. I gave her some money. It felt good and made me happy to do that. I just hope things get better for them. I don't want to hear or see them destroy themselves and their lives because I love them.

Tio Rick always bought me food and looked out for me when I would be with him. On the weekends, I played games for his teams, and he would take me to the Padres game. I always liked playing for him and being with him. So, I wished I would have started the same kind of relationship with Lucy because I know that what she is missing in life is a close family member she can trust. Not that I ever really talked to Rick about anything personal. I just loved being around him, hearing him crack jokes and talk about people at the gigs. I miss those days helping him set up and break down the equipment, running back and forth to his car for stuff or letting him know what kind of food and beers they would have, getting it for him and my dad. He's a hardworking man with a big heart. I wish he had more to show for it.

Well, there is always something going on in our family. Always good and always bad and everything in between. We never know what tomorrow brings or what the future holds. All we know is what we want to remember, but we still live on because even though we are blind, we can still see. We can see our faults, failures, achievements, and success. But, we never see each other's inner thoughts. I hope all is well when you get this, and you continue to take care for yourself and enjoy the good times. After all, that's what makes life worth living.

Playground Injury

Whenever someone leaves my dad in charge of kids, it never turns out well. Ralph lives in a one-bedroom apartment in Chula Vista, with every room connecting to the other—the bathroom to the bedroom, the bedroom to the kitchen, and the kitchen to the living room. There is no hallway. The broomstick of the neighbor downstairs pounds hard enough for us to feel it on the bottom of our feet. My dad returns the favor from the second floor. In the living room, an overweight television is positioned in the center. The frame is an imitation gold color, and the knobs are so gigantic, it takes two hands to turn the channel or turn up the volume.

My brother and I devour the remainder of our peanut butter sandwiches and semi-stale chips that were decent enough to eat just a few days after the expiration date. We hear a honk from downstairs, and I run to the screen door, looking down at the street. Uncle Chunky and Tio Rick squeeze themselves in the front seat of "The Boat," and my cousins in the back, Nando in the middle, while Ricky and Wicho are in each side. My feet fly down the stairs to Tio's Impala that sinks low into the ground.

"Where's your dad?" Tio Rick asks as I approach the passenger window.

"He's upstairs." I point to the second floor of the four apartment complex.

"Has he done any *mamadas* yet?" Tio Rick addresses, expecting family gossip.

"No time for *chismes*. We just came to drop off the kids. We can't be late to the gigs anymore, man. We need to make this *feria* so we won't be starving musicians." Uncle Chunky tries to rush.

"They're not going to pay us if you continue to fuck up the words to the songs *you* wrote." Tio Rick, who has all the ingredients in his car to make a Cape Cod, shakes the ice and indulges in the last of the vodka.

"Yo mama fucks up the words." Uncle Chunky mocks as he takes a pack of cigarettes from his pocket, smacks it a few times on his wrist, and proceeds to light a tobacco stick with ease.

"Don't you guys have the same mom?" I remind them with a smile.

"You know what? You're a stupid idiot." Tio Rick sums up his brother with the two redundant words.

Uncle Chunky calmly blows a puff of nicotine smoke, "At least I look better than you. You've been wearing the same blue shorts since 1970."

"Oh yeah, you're a lot better looking than me. You look like Pancho Villa, another fat Mexican with a mustache. You don't even help set up the music equipment. All you do is sit there on your ass and order everyone around. You don't move three inches." Tio Rick demonstrates by scooting over in his seat sideways.

"Look who's talking? You have the *panza* of an elephant." Uncle Chunky returns the weight joke and slaps me a high-five before letting out a Mexican screech, "Ay!"

"Now, we're on to animals? You look like a fucken walrus." Tio Rick turns to my cousins, who have been patiently waiting in the backseat, "This is why we don't spend Christmas together anymore."

"We've got to go, man!" Uncle Chunky tosses the cigarette out the window, and I put it out with my shoe.

"They can't get out unless you move first, *menso*."

"*Menso?* Weren't you the one who went drunk to your last baseball game during your senior year and struck out in the final inning?"

"I saw three balls coming at me. I thought I would hit one of them. Now that you're bringing up high school memories, should I tell your kids how you dumped your high school sweetheart? You remember Kelly, the head cheerleader and honor roll student."

"Okay, I'm getting out."

Uncle Chunky opens the door to the passenger side, "Veer, grab my hand," he extends his palm, while Ricky presses his hands into Uncle Chunky's *nalga* from behind the back seat, like pressing fingers into dough. Uncle Chunky shouts as he sluggishly gets out of the car, until his legs touch the ground, and the boys pour out like the *cucarachas* that live in Tio Rick's food cabinets.

As my uncles drive off still arguing about who is fatter and uglier, the gang and I walk across the street to a schoolyard playground, with thick, uneven sand. It's vacant, since the church kids are out for the day. In an empty parking lot, a basketball court, with no nets, has rims that slant to the side. The monkey bars, swings, and 10-foot slide are perfect for use as obstacles in a mock *American Gladiators* competition. "I want to be Nitro," Wicho squeaks as he flexes his heavy biceps.

"Then, I pick Gemini," Nando, in a higher pitch voice, adds after his brother. We match ourselves up according to speed and size. Wicho and Ricky, equally slow and equally dense, are the first to race against one another.

TJ picks up a stick that has collapsed from a tree next to the jungle gym. He slams the branch into the sand and draws a line. "This is the beginning of the obstacle course." His bulletproof eyeglasses flop on his nose. The WWF t-shirt he wears is peppered with bleach stains, and the parts of his clothes that were once black are now yucky brown. "Okay, get ready," TJ announces, adjusting the Coke bottles on his face. Wicho and Ricky step up to the line, both already breaking out in a slight sweat. "On your marks," their breaths become shorter. "Get set," they clutch their fist, "Go." Each foot sinks instantly into the sand, dashing to the first obstacle. The cousins bounce over the swing, both hold on to the chains while trying to pull their legs to the ground. Nando cheers on his relatives with animation, clapping and jumping simultaneously. He applauds for his brother, who slithers and rolls under the slope. Their pace instantly becomes slower as the obstacle grows shorter. Ricky makes his way to the bar, lugging himself up from the sand. By the time they reach the end, they both walk across and immediately collapse to the ground. "It's a tie," TJ reveals, "You both lag the same."

Nando and I take our position at the lopsided starting line. We are the fastest of the clan. When we are given the green light, I sprint and hurdle over the first swing, kicking my feet as I land. Nando is keeping up with my pace. My hands quickly climb up the monkey bars, and I lift myself up, using my shoulders extensively. Once I reach the top, I peek out of the right corner of my eye only to realize Nando has caught up and has a slight lead, although, I know my endurance will kick in at the end. I suddenly decide to plunge off the monkey bars, in order to make up for lost ground. I spring into the patchy dust, and my right ankle fully bends in and my face smashes into the pile of sand. I accidently swallow a mound of dirt, which makes me cough up bits and chunks of grains. My body is in too much pain to move, but I hear Wicho yell, "You can still catch him!" I stare at the finish line where Nando stands with his hands in the air. He won the race.

Once these fools realized I am really hurt and I am not getting up, they finally *walk* to me. Nando drops to his knees and removes the hair from my face.

"Are you okay?" He speaks softly, his voice frail and shaken.

"I'm dying!" I exaggerate, in order to get some sort of medical assistance.

The two brutes, Ricky and Wicho, drag me on my feet and hover me over on each of their shoulders, like Kellen Winslow in the overtime playoff game between the Chargers and Dolphins. I put my weight on the shoulders of my cousins, who are built like offensive linemen. Nando unties my shoelaces, gently taking my shoes off, as we begin making our way back to Ralph's apartment.

We teeter up the stairs and through the door, and I am thrown on the couch. Nando places a pillow underneath my ankle, elevating my leg and interrupting my dad, who intensely watches the *Price is Right*.

"She fell, as usual." TJ says to our dad. "She still hasn't figured out how to use her legs."

My dad rushes to the bathroom cabinet and returns with a nasty bottle of *Bolcanico*, the same disgusting stuff his father used for injured body parts. I don't know why Mexican people believe that *Bolcanico* is the cure for *everything*. The thin handheld bottle, the size of an airplane shot, is a dark color with a funky smell, like my dad's fungus feet. The liquid slides from within the glass, and my dad roughly jams the ointment into my wound, pounding at the bone that's sticking out. I was better off with my face decomposing in the sand. Ralph attempts to jerk my ankle back into place.

The last time my dad tumbled in the street from staggering home from the bar, he was dragged to urgent care. When the nurse asked if he knew how to operate a walker, wheelchair, or cane, my dad simply answered, "I've tried them all." This is the man that is operating on my ankle.

I scream louder with everyone chuckling at my expense, and I feel my blood gushing from my skin's tissue. "Quiet!" my dad demands, "this will make it feel better." He flips the bottle completely and drenches the rest of the fluid on my leg.

I bury my face in the pillow so that I may curse at the pain. I try to shift my foot away, but Ralph pulls my ankle back. "You are hurting me on purpose!" I let out an intense screech that seems to amuse my relatives, "That gross shit doesn't work."

"Don't cuss, goddamn it. Just stay still. I know what I'm doing."

"Dad, you can't even boil water." My brother reminds.

I can't help but to let out a little giggle. Nando looks down at me and grins. "You're going to be ok." He assures me as he pats my head. Ralph makes a fist with his hand and continues to mash the *Bolcanico* onto my ankle, which has grown more off balance and purple, and he never once bothers to ask about my well-being.

"Your feet are nasty," TJ plugs his nose, "they look like caveman feet."

"Get away from me." I chuckle as I try to dismiss my dad from his nursing obligations, but he doesn't obey. He continues to hammer, hit, break, and split, with my cousins still laughing. Their laughter begins to heal my wound.

Happy Late B-day, Veer! Did you ever get my last letter? I had sent it to your old house, so I'm hoping you got it. Congratulations! You made it to see twenty-eight! I knew you would. There was never a doubt in my mind. Now, let's hope all goes well for me so that I can see my twenty-eighth on the streets and not in one of these places. I had a good visit the other weekend. It felt good to spend some time with family. Plus, I got to eat some stuff I don't normally get. I eat oatmeal every now and then, or whenever I come up on a box. I put peanut butter, crushed cookies, bananas, and jelly in it. But lately, I've been saving the cake we get for dinner, and I make a little pie with all that stuff and eat it with the oatmeal.

I hope you get better soon. I'm guessing you won't be going to any clubs soon since you are out of commission with your sprained ankle. Don't worry about being pale, you always looked white. Shank!

Los Lobos huh, I'm sure you and everyone else will have a really great time filled with plenty of drinks and lots of dancing and hollering. I'm sure my dad will try his best to get out and make an appearance, and he will possibly talk Rick into going with him. Los Lobos are good humble people who enjoy putting on a good show for their fans and showing them appreciation. Maybe, someday I'll check them out. After all, I do like having a good time, and I'm sure I cannot go wrong with them.

That's good that you're enjoying work and coaching basketball so much. Gives you something to look forward to when you wake up. Hopefully, your team keeps on improving and you can make it all the way to Cox Arena. I hope you guys, or I mean girls, make it to the big game and emerge triumphantly. Victory is within grasp. Now, go and reach for it, obtain it, but if not, be proud of yourself nonetheless for putting out such a great effort. May victory be yours, best wishes on that. Go Cavers, go!

I'm always for someone putting themselves and their own priorities first instead of doing what makes everyone else happy or catering to others who just take it for granted. That's what I do. I give people a certain amount of chances or opportunities to prove themselves or at least show me that I am important to them. If they don't, then fuck it. It's time to do me.

P.S. I am sending some visiting forms for you in case you ever get a chance to make it out here. There's an extra one in case you lose one or mess up the other.

Encanto Ballpark

Rickey Henderson is the greatest stolen base runner of all time. "I'm going to be quick like him," Nando says, picking a baseball card from a Topps cardboard box he hides underneath his bed because he shares a room with his two older brothers. The card shows Henderson sliding into second base, his jersey covered in diamond dirt, his afro sticking out underneath the sides of his hard helmet. The card, sharp at all four edges, is placed in a separate plastic cover before Nando tucks it away for safeguarding.

Going to Encanto little league baseball games is the norm during my summers. The snack shack, filled with lukewarm hot dogs, jaw breaking Now and Later candies, and chilled sodas, is ran by the elderly lady, who adjusts her bifocals every time she reads the label of an item. I order five red vines and a snow cone that looks like the colorful wig of a clown, and the lady, whose skin is smooth like African silk, trudges over to get my cavity-infested purchase. She counts out my change even more slowly, before I rush to my seat on the bench for the final inning of the game.

The King sisters, Stacey and Sheryl, show off their cutoff daisy dukes and two-inch blue glitter fingernails, cheering for Nando, who is on deck. His All-Star jersey looks prim and his baseball pants are hiked to his knees. The letter E in cursive rests on the red helmet. He practices a few swings with his aluminum Louisville Slugger bat before approaching the plate. I catch sight of the scoreboard, visitors 1, home 1.

"Let's go, Nando, baby!" Stacey loudly invites to everyone in the stands to join in on the cheering.

"He don't want none!" Sheryl joins in the taunting of the opposing team.

"He's fresh meat!" Stacey shouts, referring to the tiresome southpaw pitcher, his legs looking like a yo-yo on the mound.

"You tell 'em girlfriend," my dad spits into my snow cone. Not wanting it to go to waste, I offer the rest to TJ. "Are you sure you don't want it?" he questions.

"Naw, I got my red vines," I replied, waving the licorice in my hand. TJ gladly accepts my spit-flecked cone.

"Vera, I can see the King sisters' *nalgas* through their shorts." Tio Rick verbally expresses his deep inner thoughts, "I bet you they are *borrachas* too."

"Goddamn it, Rick. All you ever think of is ass and booze. Can you be civilized for one damn day and pay attention to the game? Our nephew is up." Aunt Virgie swears at her brother, a spiritual ritual that has been performed since she was left to babysit her younger siblings, while their parents went to work in the humid fields of Blythe.

Nando marches to the batter box, taps his club twice on the ground, and squats. The pitcher hurls a baseball in a straight line. Nando tips it out of play. The ball flies to the stands. Another fastball attempts to cross home. "Ball!" the umpire hollers.

"Attack the strike zone!" The opposing coach yells from the dugout, "Challenge the hitter!"

Having heard the coach, Uncle Chunky, who is a spectator, counters the coach, "You need to have your swing already in motion when you see the pitcher haul his arm back." Nando gives a slight nod and adjusts his position, making his grip tighter and stance lower.

"Hey batter-batter, swing batter-batter."

The bat connects with the ball, traveling to right field. Nando reaches first base and rounds to second. My voice cracks as I cheer. The King sisters cling to and shake the fence behind home plate. My dad stomps his feet on the bleachers, causing TJ to spill half the snow cone on his shirt. Uncle Chunky uses his fingertips to whistle at the highest tone possible. The outfielder scoops up the ball and flings it to second. Nando purposely stops in his tracks, stuck in between the bases. The second baseman, who baffles with the ball, lobs it deeply over the head of the first baseman. Nando turns the bases, the ball never catching him. He tags home for an inside the park homerun. His teammates break from the dugout to embrace their MVP.

The District 42 championship banner sits at the center of the team. Nando proudly kneels in the first row. Ralph pulls out his grocery store throwaway camera. Once the team photo is complete, Ralph calls over to Nando, while the family piles around him for a memory of our own.

"Ralph, does that camera have a wide lens?" Tio Rick jokes, as we try to suck in our stomach. He flaunts his championship patch to the disposable lens. After my dad flicks the button until he runs out of pictures, I ask, "Did the coach tell you to start a pickle?"

"No. I decided to do that on my own," he admits with a happy expression, his head held high. On that summer day, Nando became Encanto's greatest base runner.

I'm glad to know my letters bring so much joy to you. It's also nice to know that you vision me by your side while reading them. Kind of makes me feel a little closer, even though we are miles apart.

It would be nice to play for the Padres. Our little season started already. All the teams are made up of inmates from the yard. We're 3-0, even though we have a few shaky players. It's a good thing the other teams have more. They didn't know about the skills until I started to unleash them. At first, I had them put me at centerfield because I thought I would get a lot of action there, but the first game I didn't get anything. So then, I had them put me at shortstop, and I've been doing my thing. I also sparked a twelve-run inning at our last at bat in the first game, with a two-man homerun. Only to get back up again with the bases loaded and put the icing on the cake with a grand slam. There are no fences, so I pretty much just have to hit it far enough to be able to round all the base. Our last game was a little close, but we still managed to pull it off. Our team ended up winning two-liter sodas each.

But now, I haven't played a game in almost three weeks because we were on lock down. It really sucked because we didn't do anything. Plus, it was during my whole two-week break from school. Maybe, I'll have a game this Saturday if we get the yard and regular program.

47

It's a good chance that I'm going to get moved out of state. I might end up moving at the end of the month if all goes well. Maybe somewhere closer to home. We shall see. Take care and try not to overwork your brain or yourself. Don't forget to turn in your visiting form next time you write.

Street Football

I am the all-time quarterback when playing street football. The football is a funky orange color that Tio Rick stole from his jobsite at the park and recreation. The football completely assembled of rubber with no threads for the grip.

The game is tied, and we form in the huddle in hopes for a game-winning drive. "Wicho, I need you to block for me while your brother goes out for a pass. Nando, I want you to go out ten yards and then cut right in front of your defender." They nod, and we clap our hands collectively. Ricky and TJ give mean eyes to their opponents. I stand in the shotgun formation, ready to take aim. The sweat is lashing out of my pores, and my deodorant has long worn off. On the snap, Ricky rams rigidly, reaching out in an attempt to grab me. I scramble to the left as Nando runs the route designed. He tracks across the street, and I launch the generic pigskin. He hooks it, dodging past TJ for a touchdown. Nando imitates a popular boogie dance, with his feet and football in hand dragging to the right and then the left. "The Icky Shuffle," Nando yells before spiking the ball.

We all pitch in to buy Nando his own rolled tacos with guacamole being the playmaker of the game. The rest of us are forced to share. We walk across the street to the Barrel, a Mexican joint where the high school kids come during school hours to grub. It is shaped like a tub, round and tall, with no place to eat inside and pigeons lurking, waiting for scraps to fall. I order our food to go, and we head back to Tio Rick's place to wash our filthy hands.

Ricky and Wicho fix the ladder that is on the side of the house. We climb to the roof to embrace in our meal, a common ritual after our street games, even though we have been warned not to do so by our elders. We stagger up the ladder one by one and plop ourselves in the middle of the sun. Nando grins as I pass him a foam plate wrapped in foil. He uncovers it, the shredded cheese melted into the crispy tortilla. "To me," he toasts, just before crunching into his food. His bites look big and satisfying, and he resembles a whale eating a school of fish.

He sees me eyeballing and points the rolled taco in my direction. I open my mouth wide, and he feeds me the final bite.

"You goddamn kids!" Tata snaps as he views us enjoying our lunch. That's his favorite words, "goddamn"—Goddamn dog, goddamn it, goddamn you. It's like that's all the vocabulary he knows, despite having been a legal U.S. citizen for over forty years. During election years, Cat goes into the booth with him to translate the documents. The other voters could hear him behind the curtain, "Goddamn it, no. Goddamn it, no!" All the propositions marked with the same answer.

Tata chases us as we climb down the ladder. We hop over the three-foot fence and scurry into the street. Tata's pants are too big for him. His watermelon stomach makes it unorthodox for normal belts to wrap around his *menudo* eating waistline, so he wears a rope that ties from the back loop to the opposite side of the front. The rope unravels during his attempt to hit us with the leather belt. Nando and I lead the pack and sprint the straightaway. Tata tumbles on the uneven pavement while still cussing, but Nando and I keep running side by side.

Yeah, I remember that. He gave me $20, and it was great. I was so happy I did that. Remember when he would ask me what family member I like better, and when I would pick the one on the Sanchez side, he would give me money. Your dad is burnt out and wild. Your dad is a funny guy, never seems to surprise me. I wonder if he got the kicking someone in the ass and then smiling from me when I was little or if I got it from him somehow. Shank!

You know he's always going to be the same old Ralph no matter what. Not too much you can say or do to change him because he won't change. We all just got to accept him and his wild tactics. You know how your dad likes to brag about things: his Master's degree, your basketball games, TJ's football games. With you getting your Master's now, he can't say he's the only Sanchez to get one. The only thing that can probably slow your dad down is a drought of tequila and beer.

I know he's a bit difficult to deal with, but I think he does it to see if we still forgive him and love him the same after it all. All I can suggest is to do the things he likes to do. Take him to Charger games, Padre games, on trips to the central valley area to visit the family he grew up with. Anywhere and anything his heart may desire. Good old Lin. Tell him I said hey, and I send my love his way.

left to right: Monchi, Ralph, Tata, Nando.

Before a ballet folklorico performance: Vera, Wicho, Cat holding Nando.

Nando was the baby of the family.

Nando always loved being with his father, Chunky.

Cat and Nando enjoying the sun, 1985.

Primos with Tata.

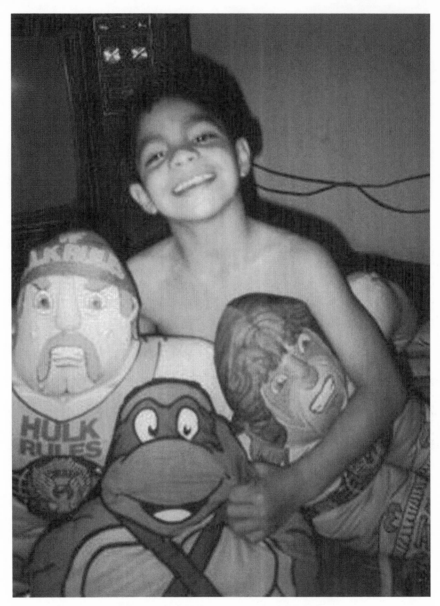

Nando with his Ninja Turtle and WWF pillows.

Nando and Wicho with Virgie's cats.

1992 MLB All-Star, San Diego Convention Center

School picture at Encanto Elementary.

Nando sneaking in the picture.

Nando and siblings, Esmi and Monchi.

Nando playing for Encanto Little League.

Nando graduating from O'Farrell Junior High.

Charger playoff game, 1995.

Portrait of Tata, Artist De Los Reyes.

Nando with his cousins and brothers at Chunky's gig.

Mission Bay High School football, 2000.

Winning the Division III C.I.F. championship game at Qualcomm Stadium.

Nando looking sharp at his high school prom.

Nando graduating with honors from Garfield High School.

left to right: Rick, Ralph, Nando, and Chunky at Chiquitas Restaurant.

Rick and Chunky singing at Nando's graduation party.

Pick a Side

My dad has a tendency to blow all his money within a few days of getting paid. "You're driving," Ralph says as he wiggles the keys in my face. It's always reassuring when he doesn't drive. Once, he did a hit-and-run on his brother's car, while backing out of the driveway. Tio Rick stared from his apartment window as my dad banged into the "boat," and then sped off without leaving a note and thinking he wouldn't see his brother again.

I take the keys, opening the trunk of the car, carelessly throwing my backpack and basketball beside his dirty laundry. The practice jersey I wear should be in the pile. I slam the door to the used blue Nissan vehicle and adjust the seat to fit my vertically challenged frame. The cloth interior peeling at the roof and the windshield wiper is missing on the passenger side. I see Mission Bay cheerleaders practice their backflips and complete pyramid form, and the jocks lift heavily in the weight room. I position the key in the ignition. As I start the engine, Ralph suggests we go visit his favorite brother—whichever brother doesn't kick him out of their house that week is his favorite.

After exiting the 94 freeway, we stop by Ken's liquor store for a quick slammer. We gradually get out of the car, and I place the keys in the pocket of my Nike basketball shorts, knowing I will be the designated drive for the remainder of the evening. Inside, hot dogs revolve in a Ferris wheel-style machine, and Mama K's brownies, at $1 a pop, are tidily stacked in a bamboo basket. I take a Gatorade from the fridge, a pack of chewing gum from the shelf, and place them both on the counter. Ralph, who just made a money order for the rent, taps his foot on the floor with his shoes that are missing shoelaces. He sucks his teeth, unsure what size he desires. "Give me a large." Ralph never seems to disappoint me. Ken, the blubbery Chaldean with a receding hairline, turns around to face the lineup of hard liquor. He places the vodka in the brown paper bag, while my dad hands him a bank issued ten-dollar bill. We get into the automobile bucket and head up the hill to Radio Drive, paying a visit to Uncle Chunky and the rest of the *bola*.

Without wasting any time, Ralph untwists the cap to the plastic bottle that is still in the brown bag, and pours the Russian drink down his tonsils. The container instantly becomes half-empty, and the quench of an eager mouth becomes satisfied.

As I reach the top of the hill, I ease off the gas and lightly place my foot on the break, coasting to my uncle's house. There is no sidewalk in front, so I roughly pull up to a curb filled with shattered rocks and nuggets. Nando and a few of his siblings are outside, taking in the upbeat rays of the unforgiving sun. His black SD cap is backwards, and his long white shirt sags past his knees. The shoelaces to his shell toe Adidas remain purposely untied.

I step out of the car and go down the stairs to the base of the ground that leads to the front yard, in order to embrace my youngest cousin. My dad throttles as he gets out and shoves the plastic bottle in his raggedy shorts that were purchased for fifty cents at a yard sale. "Nando, everyone likes Nando," my dad says, a phrase my dad recites every time he sees his nephew. He staggers but tumbles on the second step. His ankle twists and his knees smack the concrete. His arms stretch out as if he were sliding into home plate, and his bottle of vodka pops out from his shorts. I laugh hard enough that I clamp my stomach and lean on my cousin because I cannot hold myself up. The rest of the gang joins me in tears of amusement. This causes Ralph to yell for help even louder.

Nando walks over and extends his hand to his uncle, who lies in an exaggerated pose on the ground. Ralph merely lifts his upper body and drags his legs while Nando brings him to his feet. He dusts off Ralph's Viva Las Vegas shirt. Grateful for the kind gesture, he pulls out a clean twenty-dollar bill, and gives it to Nando, whose smile is now bigger when the fall occurred. Continuing with his generous spirit, Ralph quizzes, "Little Child, Little Child, we're going to play a game. I'm going to ask you ten questions, and if you get the answers correct, I will give you a dollar. Who are the relatives you like better the Sanchez or the *other side*? Nando grins as to accept his offer. "Who do you like better, me or the nasty Indian, from the *other side*?"

"You." My dad slaps him his first dollar.

"Who do you like better, Tio Rick or Larry the Leach?"

Nando gives a chuckle before answering, "Tio Rick." Another dollar is handed his way.

"Who do you like better, your favorite fat Aunt Virgie or Aunt *Trompas*, with armpit hairs so hairy you can braid them and with teeth so big you can feed her an apple through a gate?"

Taking a chance, Nando replies, "Huh, Virgie?" Ralph sucks his teeth and hesitates to give him a dollar but eventually does.

"She is my favorite sister, you know." Ralph explains.

"Isn't she your only sister?" I add to the questions.

"Let's continue. Who do you like better, TJ or Chato, who still plays with Barbies?" The pile of currency increases in Nando's hand.

"Who do you like better, Vera or Rat Face? Chunky used to pay Vera five cents to pinch her when they were little because she was so ugly." We both smile.

"This is the magic question, so it's worth ten dollars. Who do you like better, your father or *her*? And remember, there is a right answer."

Every time Nando picked a relative on the Sanchez side, he earned one more dollar. Nando emerges with a handful of cash and my dad with an empty wallet.

It's crazy how when we go a little while without doing something we like, that we know we are good at and enjoy doing, that it feels so good and wish we wouldn't have gone so long without doing it. It's just a great sensation that you don't want to end. Like a couple of weeks ago, I was playing catch with a real baseball, and it was a great feeling I hadn't felt in a long time. It was much fun just catching and throwing. All I could think about was how I can't wait to play with all my nephews and show them how to throw a curve or not be afraid to field the ball and use techniques.

I think you should utilize your talents more and share them with the world. I talked to my dad and said he's been busy working like crazy to do the Cesar Chavez holiday,

73

but I'm sure he enjoys it. We might be poor, but not stupid. We develop to who we are by what we are exposed to and based on the decision we make. Unfortunately, some are exposed to harsher living environments, causing confusion and misunderstanding. Others have a much clearer path, with not so many difficult obstacles. There's no doubt that you should never blame the child, but that doesn't mean all the blame goes on the parent when society itself is cruel and influences everyone in it. Some for the good and some for the worse.

It usually takes about 8 hours to get housed. Just because someone is locked up, it doesn't make or mean they are a bad person, just misfortunate. The D.A. is pretty tricky and cutthroat. They don't like to lose, but yet somehow always manage to let some people get off pretty easy. Sometimes, I expect the worse but hope for the best. Some psychologists are very arrogant and quick to judge on appearance. Depending on the situation, I like to play with them when I see them, especially if I can tell their funny style. It is never easy to be fully at peace or even close to it, especially with the days that can make my worst thought come true. I like having a busy schedule because it keeps me from thinking about my time, but at night, before I go to sleep, it will cross my mind, and it makes me feel uncomfortable. I will keep my head up, making it through everything positively. That's the best way I can do it.

Undefeated Record

This was my first time wearing my varsity lettermen jacket after graduating high school. My dad bought it for me as a Christmas present when I lettered as a freshman in track and later in basketball. On the back, a patch of a Buccaneer clenches a knife in his mouth, and my last name appears above the mascot my favorite lettering, Old English. At times, I can be a typical Mexican.

We decorate banners for the championship game. I use the pattern on my jacket to design my picture, adding the numbers 55 and 58 on each side of the Buc. Ralph smears the lettering across the print with his left hand, making the characters disproportionate and unsymmetrical. Once the paint dries, I roll up my poster and strap on a rubber band, and we rush to the car, speeding over to Qualcomm Stadium.

My dad and I maneuver our way to field level, where we see Cat and Wicho anticipating the start of game. "Tio, come over here!" Cat gestures for us to sit next to the rest of family. Aunt Virgie stuffs a handful of nachos in her mouth, although most of the sauce falls on her shirt, "Don't invite him over here."

"Gobble gobble and wobble wobble, Virgie. You might want to give your teeth a break before the game starts."

"At least I have teeth. You have no teeth, no hair, and no ass."

"Virgie, do you eat anything that moves?"

"Ralph, you think drinking is a goddamn marathon. You and the Rolling Stones are living proof that you can abuse your body and still live."

"*Como chingan esos dos*. Do you two ever give it a break?" Tio Rick asks as he observes the stadium through the binoculars.

"I thought dad would be here by now?" Wicho ponders to Cat, who is taking pictures of the stadium.

"I spoke to him at five this morning. He said he was going to come. Maybe something changed." Ralph spits.

A man with a gleeful newscaster voice announces, "Ladies and gentlemen, welcome to the Division III title game. Today, the Mission Bay Buccaneers look to secure their undefeated streak for the first time in school history, but they must first get past the Lincoln Hornets!" The fans on both sides of the football field roar at the broadcast. "This will definitely go down in the books, so hold on to your seats!"

The MB football players dart out of the tunnel and through the immense sign that reads, "Western League Champs." They wear their all-black uniforms, ready for battle. The black and yellow helmets are Riddell brand, just like the pros. Nando and TJ jog on the turf to prepare for kickoff.

***

"It's first and goal for Lincoln. Facemask penalty on Mission Bay. Lincoln, trying to add to their lead. QB Swanson runs, trying to take it in himself, but fumbles the ball. Mission Bay's Marcus Smith recovers the football! Marcus Smith taking it back for Mission Bay! Marcus Smith will he go? Senior #25, Shannon Nowden, takes out two Lincoln defenders to assist with the play. This is high school football, folks. The 6'4, 205 pound junior Smith goes the distance for 95 yards for the tying touchdown. Eder Mendoza handles the kicking chores of MB, giving them a one-point lead in the first quarter. Mendoza boots the ball back deep into Lincoln territory. Corey Jones is there for the catch. He goes outside, but he is shoved out of bounds by sophomore, Fernando Sanchez."

***

One minute left on the clock. "A handoff to Jaja Riley. Riley with a spin move and gets a few yards ticking down the remaining seconds of a Mission Bay victory." Ralph and I flap our signs in the air. The MB players butt heads with their helmets and begin the countdown to victory. TJ and Nando make their way to the family while Ralph hurdles over the rail and nearly tackles his son from excitement.

During his college years, Ralph ran on the football field with the San Diego State marching band during the halftime show. The musician handed him the drumsticks. Ralph banged the instrument and stomped to the fight song before being tossed over the railing by security.

Cat and I hug Nando. He reeks of funky sweat, his jersey drenched and sticky. I look at him, his eyes a bit drained, scanning the audience. "Sanchez and Sanchez," Coach Pugh mandates, "get your asses over here so we can take this team picture." The players huddle at center field, with the scoreboard repeatedly twinkling, C.I.F. Champs! C.I.F. Champs! The fireworks explode and dissolve in the sky, while newspaper reporters trying to maneuvers their way to an interview. Coaches already dress in their preordered championship t-shirts stand behind their players. Nando glances at the ground and then at his cousin. TJ, who points his index finger in the air, places an arm around Nando. "1-2-3- Undefeated!" A perfect football season, with lettermen jackets that tell a story that'll go down in school history.

Go Cavers! You ladies did it and with a little style, it seems. They are most definitely strong and mature for their age. I enjoyed reading the article. I'm sure your plaque is nice. Maybe one day, you can be head coach.

I remember playing for the C.I.F. title with your brother at Qualcomm Stadium. I had a big argument with my parents that morning, ran off up the hill around the way, started smoking some weed. Like always, I cried up a storm while contemplating death. I almost missed the bus to the stadium. I got there right before we started loading up. During the whole game, my mind was somewhere else. It was like the game didn't even matter to me. I even missed a punting play I was supposed to be in, and Coach Pugh didn't like that at all. After everything, all the games and stuff, I was alone with no one but Mary Jane. I caught the trolley home. Then, I walked home from the trolley with my CIF patch in my pocket, with it meaning nothing to me.

A week before that, I was downtown, doing my thing. I was hoping on the trolley back to 32nd and Commercial, but as I'm getting on the trolley, a smoker gets my attention and tells me to get off, so I do. I go handle my business. I finish then catch the first blue line to the 12th and Imperial to wait for the next Orange Line. While I'm waiting, an announcement comes over the speakers, saying that there was a homicide at 32nd and Commercial, so the Orange Line will only go to 25th. I get off and start walking to 32nd down Imperial Ave. I then see a group of my homies and ask what happened. They tell me one of the little homies from the turf got shot and died at the trolley, while another homie from the neighborhood got shot and survived. So if I never would have gotten off the original trolley I was on, I could have been there during the time the shooting took place.

There comes a time when a child's innocence is vanquished. For there is a young mind trying to live up to the standards of not only their peers but those of their parents. Along that line is where one gets lost and loses focus on what's really best for their future. Not all of them have the proper guidance or good upbringing, and even though they all have a choice to persist, many fall into their natural cycle of life due to being ignored and not taken into consideration. The good thing about life is that we all get the opportunity to bounce back one way or the other. We just need that one good wake up call. Sooner or later, what someone does in the dark always comes to light. Then, we must continue to stay strong and fight for what we want for our goals, for the better life we want to lead. We cannot be afraid to seek help, but most importantly, we cannot be afraid to let those know who need help that we are here to help them in their time of need. Many of us want and need help with life, but all of us are afraid to ask for it in some point in our lives. As for me, life goes on, and I must continue to take the good with the bad. I have plans to be better off, just got to stay more focused on the bigger picture. I put up with a lot because it's the only way I will be able to make it where I'm trying to get to, closer to home.

Cheese and Eggs for Breakfast

The sizzling sound of bacon on the stove is enough for me to wake up with a smile on my face. I rotate my neck from side to side, embracing the crackles in my joints. I lay my crusty feet in the Winnie the Pooh slippers that I bought for five bucks at the local swap meet and zip to the kitchen. I tiptoe behind Nando, whose shorts fall below his waistline, while the do-rag keeps his elongated hair from crawling into the food. He scrambles the eggs with red bell peppers and chops them into tiny pieces with a wooden spatula. Being the youngest, he relishes to creatively feed himself. He flips the yolk in the air repeatedly, catching all the ingredients in the slippery pan. Lately, Nando has been coming over my place across town. I don't mind it one bit because I like the company.

I settle my hands on both biceps that seem to be strong enough to perform bench presses and push-ups during the off-season, yet are gentle enough to crack the embryo of a chicken. "My favorite fellow," I reveal with a smile. The salt and pepper simmer in the potatoes, and the buttermilk pancakes are stacked in layers, ready for us to chow down on them.

"Veer the beer," he warmheartedly pokes fun at my nickname and turns off the flames at the same time. I remove the paper plates from the cabinet, and Nando kindly serves our grub. I cart our dishes to the coffee table in the living room, and Nando follows with two glasses of country style orange juice.

Before we get comfortable, I read the title of numerous VHS and DVDs, to serve as entertainment during our meal. "I haven't seen the *Nutty Professor II*," Nando announces while pouring syrup on his fluffy pancakes. "Good choice," I have always been a Janet Jackson fan, whether it be her movies or music. In fourth grade, my friends and I were the opening act to the talent show. We performed Janet's "Escapade," wearing all black, just as she did in her videos.

I insert the movie into the VHS and fast-forward the previews to the opening scene in a church. Professor Klump is preparing to recite his vows to Denise, Janet's character. My fork digs into my *papas* as I eat the starch first, my favorite. My stomach delighted with every savory bite. Grandma Klump drives into the church on her scooter, running over the foot of an extra. As she strolls to the front aisle and parks her motor, she executes the sign of the cross, kisses her lips, and raises her hand to the sky. Nando and I burst, almost choking on our food, and mimic the gesture.

"How is it?"

"Amazing." I answer in one word.

"I cook for myself all the time. Some food I learned to cook from Cat, but most of them, I pretty much learned on my own. I was thinking of entering culinary school after high school," Nando adds, before taking a sample of the eggs.

I pause to look into his eyes. They are serious and truthful.

"Chef Nando. I like the sound of that."

I raise my cup of orange juice, and Nando does the same. We bang the glasses and propose a toast to the master chef-to-be.

I wish I could be out for the family reunion. It's like a once-in-a-lifetime event, and I won't be able to experience it. Did someone videotape it for those, like me, who can't make it? Sounds like a whole lot of family for me to meet, catch up with and also remember. Tia Lupe wasn't there? She's one I will never forget. You know we sure do know how to have a good time with a couple of mamadas in the mix. We wouldn't be us if we didn't, sort of like a trademark. It makes all the gatherings more memorable.

Thank you for trying to send me the magazines, but I can't get anything with nudity, so that means Playboy and stuff like it. As long as they are covered up, nipples and the privates, it's all good. I'll count it as my Christmas and birthday present, so you can kill two birds with one stone.

Last week was my first time ever being in the snow. I always planned on going to the snow or somewhere where it snows but as a free man. People were making snowmen and having snow fights. At night during chow, two black guys were paid to tackle the snowmen in their boxers. There were three big ones. They double-teamed the biggest one and then took out one on their own. Everybody was cheering, hollering, and laughing. It would have been a great hit on YouTube.

As for everything else, it's pretty much the same old, same old. Just patiently and anxiously waiting for my counselor to do what he said he would do, so I could go back to camp. If all goes well, maybe February, I'll be back at camp, so let's keep our fingers crossed. There are a lot of men's fitness magazines floating around here, so I'm able to get some helpful tips out there. I'm going back to my Burpees and pull-ups, also dips, and I lift a sandbag we made. But, I spread it out more now, and I don't try to do it all in one day. That way, I don't burn myself out or strain my body. Gotta make sure I'm healthy and don't have any injuries, so I can make it back to camp.

The First Time

What happens in Vegas stays in Vegas, but once coming home, everything turns back into reality. I park my Ford Ranger on the street and unload my duffle bag from the tailgate. I walk down the alley and open the wooden gate to my house, one of three on the lot. I go inside and leave my luggage by the door entrance because at the moment, I don't feel like unpacking my clothes. Water sounds tasty to anyone who was in Vegas for their twenty-second birthday, so I head to the kitchen to chug on an icy bottle. Through the window, I spot Nando at the back door, waiting. *Did I tell him when I would return?* I let him inside the house, and Nando turns on the T.V. and video games immediately.

"How long were you waiting for me?" Ignoring my question, Nando shrugs his shoulders and pays attention to the screen.

Not thinking much about it, I return to my room and plop on the bed to reminisce about the trip, when I am immediately interrupted by a stern knock on the front door. A sigh comes from deep within my chest, and I roll off my bed to answer the door. Nando beats me to the door, but he leaves outside to meet a butch lady, who I briefly catch a glimpse of through the cracks of the door. She looks tough—boyish blonde hair, 501 jeans, comfortable jogging shoes, and a thick watch, which only reads in military time. She's in clothing that doesn't need to impress her boss because she *is* the boss. She helps herself to opening my door wider, and I stand there a bit confused. She must have notice my clouded expression.

"Do you live here?" Her voice sounds sour and strict.

"Yes, come in," and I hunker on the couch, even more puzzled.

"I am Detective Mason," she flashes her polished badge, a symbol of supreme authority. "How do you know this young man here?" She points to Nando, who frowns, returning to sit on the love seat.

"He's my younger cousin. Can you tell me what's going on? I just got in from out of town," I replied, gesturing towards my bags near the entry.

"There was a situation at the 76 gas station a few blocks from here. Your cousin and another juvenile held up the gas station. Your cousin was the lookout, keeping an eye out for the cops. He left the scene during the holdup, but we were able to catch the other suspect. He led us back here. They were both here prior to the robbery, apparently all weekend, while you were gone. The cashier at the gas station gave us a very *accurate* description of the two boys. We found this in the other suspect's wallet." She holds a current Mission Bay High School ID.

"Can I search the house for weapons and guns?" I give her permission to do so. She investigates the cabinets, drawers, and other odd places, but she comes out empty handed. Nando flusters, gazing at the floor. I could tell he is disappointed with his actions and regrets his poor decision making.

"What's your phone number? I am going to inform your parents of the robbery." The detective picks up the phone and dials. The witch with the evil voice answers. Cries on the other end of the line can be clearly understood.

The detective enlightens my cousin as she hangs up the phone. "I'm going to release you to your cousin because she's old enough, but she is taking you straight home. Your parents are waiting. I do believe there is hope for you."

I drive Nando in my gray pickup. We remain silent on the drive, and he continues to sit frozen, like a child waiting to see the warden. As we arrive at Radio Drive, Uncle Chunky is outside on the porch, smoking a cigarette, forcefully puffing in the nicotine. He doesn't say much when we get out of my truck. *She* waddles outside with a grandkid on her hip. *She* hysterically hollers into our ears, like fingernails on a chalkboard. He lets *her* rant and rave about how he is an embarrassment, "How could you do this to me? You better not feel sorry for yourself! Don't you dare!" Nando continues to stay silent, which he has been for a few hours now. During this humiliation, he doesn't speak, but I know all his repulsive childhood memories return.

I know I've been hurting a lot of people, losing people I love and not only disappointing them, but also embarrassing them. I know what it feels like to lose yourself, lose love, and what's important. Sometimes, losing something really opens your eyes. When you have something that's great, at first you realize it. Then, after a while, you forget about it or feel as if no matter what, you're always gonna have it and it ain't going nowhere. So, you start taking it for granted and acting as if it doesn't mean what it used to. Everyone is always gonna look at you different when you do something so out of left field. Only because they think they know you. Just know that I will never look at you different or think about you differently. That's because I realize where you come from and understand that the way you came up had its benefits but also a lot of negatives.

The same goes for me, though. I realize at times I can be patient and calm about things and not let things affect me. I get that from my dad. But, I also feel like I'm never satisfied, always wanting more. And I get that from my mom. In the end of it all, I'm still my own person and make my own decisions. I'm glad I helped you grow or open yourself more to the harsh realities of this world. I know I touched you in a way that was for the better, but I'm sorry for making you cry.

I shall continue to stay open, never holding back. I shall continue to help through my letters. Some people fear life; some people fear death. I think that to fear nothing at all is the true test. To be able not to fear anything in this world or out of this world.

The Trolley Stop

The Padres came back to beat the Dodgers in the bottom of the ninth inning as Trevor Hoffman marches on the field to secure the game. The fans rise from their seat as hells bells sounds over the speakers. TJ and I crush peanut shells underneath our feet as we leap from our seats, with the rest of Petco Park. The Friar dances the twist with a mother and her child, all of which is captured on the Jumbotron. The Beatles' version of "Twist and Shout" keeps the boosters wild before Hoffman fires his final strike, clinching the ballgame.

We jump on the escalator to the ground level and head out of the ballpark, as the Pad Squad hands out coupons for free tacos at a nearby fast food restaurant. The crowd, flowing like a herd of cows, crosses the street and head to the Gaslamp Headquarters for more late night excitement. TJ and I pass by the trolley station, and I surprisingly see Nando sitting by himself on a bench, waiting as if he has nowhere else to go. A crowd of Padres fans tumble pass him, and for a moment, it appears as if he is hidden. He sports a winter jacket, and a dark beanie covers his eyebrows. His hands remain tucked away in the pockets, and he quickly eyes everyone that walks by. TJ and I approach our cousin, who is elated to see us in return, but he keeps the conversation short when we try to speak to him.

"Did you go to the game?"

"Naw. Did we win?

"Yes, Trevor Hoffman was clutch in the last inning. He will for sure be another future Hall of Famer." I predict. I traveled to Cooperstown the year Ozzie Smith was inducted, and returned to San Diego with too many souvenirs, shot glasses for my dad and uncles, and a baseball book for myself that I read while on the airplane home. I am confident Hoffman will join the elite baseball players someday.

"That's tight."

"Where are you going?" Nando shakes his head, to leave the answer open ended. I offer, "Do you want a ride?" He shakes his head again and refuses, his lips chapped and pale. "It's not a problem. I'll take you wherever you need to go." For a third time, he denies me, and I can see something missing in his eyes. He is misplaced. There was only one explanation for why he didn't want a ride, and I soon began to answer my own question.

"Are you sure?" TJ does his best to convince Nando.

"Naw. I'll be cool."

As we walk away from Nando, I turn to notice his figure lower into his jacket, unmoved, his eyes silent, and his body slowly becomes invisible.

As you know by now, I never ended up going out of state, which is good, but I still relocated to another temporary place of residence. It's called Jamestown, and it's in Sacramento. I chose to come here so that I can go through the firefighting program so I may go to fire camp and fight wild fires once I successfully complete the training. It is a little bit better from where I was, but it's still prison. The good thing is that I already started one portion of the training, and should be complete by next Friday. It's the physical training part. We do a lot of power walking and running. We do it in a certain amount of time. It's to get us ready for the mountain hiking. If all goes well, I will probably be shipped off to a camp by the end of March, at least I'm hoping. I finally got my property that they misplaced earlier this week, so I have your address again. I know it's been awhile since you heard from me, and I apologize for that. I heard Ricky was still doing pretty good. I hope he keeps it together. Your brother needs to realize that he is important to us as we are to him. That no matter how long he stays away, no matter how much he might hate or despite our ways and the way we are as individuals, we are still family. We will all love each other unconditionally. There's nothing stronger than family, but there are always things that appear to be. I wouldn't change it for the world nor would I change who we are. Some might say that love is the key to happiness. I like to think that family is the key to love.

I'm trying to get real solid. I max out at 285 lbs. I'm trying to get to 300 lbs. in a week or two, probably two. We be balling like every weekend, sometimes full court if we have enough people that ain't lazy. Another summer is here; came kind of quick for me. This summer, however, I will be working and doing more than I've done in the past two. Five days a week from 8:30 am to 4:00 pm, some days easier than others and some shorter as well as longer. Still waiting to go on my first big campaign. We call them "out of counties." That's where the real money is, for us at least. There is nothing wrong with relaxing; everyone needs rest and relaxation. Too much over working your mind and body isn't good, but sometimes necessary. There's always room for improvement for all of us, even it's just a little bit. I plan on traveling someday, just got to get situated and my priorities up to par. The camp has its benefits, but it's still modern slavery. If you don't do your part, then you're gone, but that's the way it is in the real world. Survival of the fittest. I am looking at it like it's getting me ready and improving my work ethic and capability. I'm also making sure to enjoy the fruits of labor. Plus, it helps make the time pass. Always able to keep busy and not think of the dates. I shall continue to push forward and prevail. For I am the only one that can hold myself back or keep myself down. So forward is the only way because time doesn't allow us to move back and change where we already are. Adios, hasta luego, from your favorite fellow.

Timed Talk

"Nando, everybody likes Nando! How are things going inside?"

"I'm cool. I was at Tio Rick's house the other day. Your dad was meeting him there to go to a gig. My dad showed up, and according to Tio Rick, was getting in the way. "

"Your dad said my dad looked like Pappy."

"Popeye's dad. Tio Rick said he would pay to get the gross beard shaved."

"Of course he said something back. He called your dad Humpty Dumpty and then farted."

"Tio Rick sprayed his ass with air freshener right before The Virg walked in."

"The Virg had to take them to the gig. She is the only one with a valid driver's licenses, no DUI, and a car that works."

"She complained, and then my dad asked her how come diets don't work for her."

"She asked him when was he going to die."

"She said she would rather be fat than an alcoholic. She reminded him that he's the one who got carried out of the Charger game on a stretcher and was taken away in an ambulance."

"Because he fell and smacked his head on the rail when we scored a touchdown."

"I picked him up."

"Multiple choice question. Did he, A: go get his medication, B: go home, C: take a nap, or D: go to the bar after he was release from the hospital."

"Ding! Ding! Ding! You're right."

"You need to go? That was quick. When do you think you will be allowed to call again?"

"Ok, I'll be waiting."

Well, as you now, I have been moved once again. This place is the best thus far out of all the others. Much more freedom and much easier to do time. I'm still waiting to start the next and final stage of the firefighting training so that I can complete it and get shipped off to a camp. It's going on three weeks and still nothing. My time will come soon enough, no reason to worry. It's relaxing and easygoing here. The food is more edible and plentiful. The TV's have plenty selections of channels. We have a Ping-Pong table, a pool table, an all right basketball court, small hand court, and last but not least, a weightlifting area that I tend to take full advantage of. The softball field is pretty small, though and no one has played since I've been here.

I think it's because fire season started, plus, inmates are usually tired from coming back from work during the week. That's the down side. We usually do lots of laboring, but that's the price we pay for such a better living condition. Right now, all the other crews have gone to Santa Barbara for the big fire. The reason our crew is the only one here is because our captain was sick this past week, so he pussied out on taking us out of county. I've been on a couple of fires already, but they were small. They are known as crack fires. We got a fine meal for it, double bacon cheeseburger with the works, fries, Minute Made canned drink, and ice cream. Very fulfilling and delicious. One of the benefits of going on a fire, not to mention the $1 an hour. It's pretty much nothing, but hey, it's better than nothing. Every little bit helps, you know. Plus, it will add up at the end of the season. I just got to try and not gain too much weight because they got a lot of pastries for dessert. Like I said, it is real cool here, and I enjoy it a lot.

That's cool you and Virgie had a nice pleasant outing. Did you do the Y-M-C-A dance? Or did you sing along to Amy Winehouse's "Rehab" with the rest of the pride parade? It was probably good for both of you, for giving her something positive and fun to do with her niece. For you, giving you break from your busy life and being able to enjoy it with your aunt, who you don't get to spend a lot time with. It's about being content with yourself and also with what you have done, accomplished and happiness and whether or not you can find it, grasp it, notice it's there, and hold on to it for as long as you can.

The Phone Call

"Nando is dead." The words hit me fast without warning. Aunt Virgie cries to me over the phone, her voice filled with discomforting tears, and I can practically see the tears pouring down her face.

"What do you mean?" I throb, as my blood slowly begins to feel colder. The first death Nando and I experienced was when our grandmother died of cancer in the red house. I was only eight, and she passed away in front of us, gasping her final breath as she suffered in bed. Then, when I was a freshman in high school, our grandfather died. He had suddenly stopped eating, drinking, and caring Even then, at those ages, I could cope, but this was entirely different. This was Nando's death. This, I cannot understand.

"He died in an automobile accident." My mind still fumbles over the simple words that form in the most complicated sentence I've ever heard, *Nando is dead*. The moment I never believed would arrive is here. I am foolish for thinking that the truth is not a reality. Then it gradually hits me that Nando is no longer with us. "What are you thinking?" Aunt Virgie tries to collect my thoughts, although I am aware that she cannot gather hers.

"I don't know." I reply, and I truly mean it. His death was a sure promise to me, a guaranteed fate that tangles in my mind, while the pounding of my heart does most of the talking. Aunt Virgie and I remain quiet, as the phone drops from my hand, and Nando drifts out of our lives.

***

I rush to my truck and drive to Tio Rick's apartment. He lives just down the street, so I am there in minutes, and my dad waits at the gate of the apartments. When I approach him, he sinks his head into my shoulder and lets out loud sobs. I can't cry; I just hold him. We go inside the apartment, and I find that Tio Rick is teary eyed, too. The television is on, and the incident is being covered on the news.

"A deadly crash occurred today around two o'clock when a Milton Bacon, a resident of Nevada, collided with a boxy fire truck that was carrying multiple minimum security inmates. Fernando Julio Sanchez was part of a firefighter crew returning to their post when he and other inmates were ejected from the truck upon impact. CHP is not sure what caused Bacon to hit the truck that was driving eastbound. Sanchez was the only fatality from the crew. He was pronounced dead at the scene." I blink back the tears, his short life filled with too many unpleasant memories, which made his life seem longer. My dad, who is rambunctious and lively, and Tio Rick, who is sarcastically humorous, sit frozen and only the bitter night speaks. I realize this is what it means to be human. This is what it feels like to let Nando go.

The real world can be pretty demanding. Just try to stay on top of it because it's even harder trying to play catch up when you already have a lot on your plate. Just try to get the rest when the opportunity presents itself because it's the essential way to live.

As for me, I'm not at camp anymore, but I'm all right, though. I got rolled up for some bullshit, and I would have been sent to another camp already, but my points are too high. When I went to camp clarification, they told me I wasn't even supposed to be at camp because my points were already too high, but somehow I slipped through. Now, I got to wait until November for my points to drop down, but if I get written up, then I end up going back to a three yard. If I can make it until then being disciplinary free, then I'll go back to camp, but it will be a different one. So we will have to wait and see.

When I was in camp, I would lift weights on Monday, Wednesday, and Friday. I try to run at least three miles throughout the week. I would usually hike the back hill every day and then ball after that. But now, since we don't have weights here, I do Burpees; there are various ways to do them. The type I like to do are called "Navy Seals."

Basically, I run in place, then go down in the push up position, do one push up, then kick my knees to my chest, while I'm in the up position. Then, I do another push up, kicking my knees to my chest again with the opposite leg. Then, I do another push up, then hop back up to my feet, do three squats, and start running in place again. I wait for my partner to do his. I do that 100 times just going back and forth in a steady rhythm. Sometimes, I don't have a partner do to them with me, but I still do them on my own. I try to do those every day of the week, along with 100 pull ups, 200 dips, and an extra 200 or 300 incline push-ups. I do that during yard time, but not on Sundays. I haven't been running lately, but I need to start doing it. I need to start ballin' again, too. I only played one day since I've been back. We played five games, and we won all of them. I'm about to start this fiber optic course soon as I go back to my class. I should be done by July and get another certificate.

I called dad's house to check in and let them know I'm okay and what's going on with me. I write them every now and then, too. When I called three weeks ago, I was able to catch Tio Rick and talk to him for a little bit. Tia Virgie was there another time I called, and we spoke briefly. I talked to Esmi and Wicho today for the first time in a while. I'm hoping I can get what I need to get done this coming week. Hopefully, next time I write you back, I'll be able to tell you I'm on my way back to camp.

Uncle Chunky's Voice

"The man on the other line said the words I fear, 'I regret to inform you.' After that, I heard nothing because I knew. I just knew. I didn't need to hear anything else. Nando was changing, becoming more spiritual and ready to move forward with his life. That's what he wrote to me in his letters home. He had a cellmate, a Native-American, elder, much wiser. He gave Nando words of wisdom and shared with him the indigenous ways and taught him to heal through spiritual release, rather than anger and frustration. When Nando was done with his time, he and I were going to leave, together. We had plans to escape, to live far away from here. Do you remember when the detective went over your house when you lived in P.B.? The cashier testified against him in court, and the cashier said he knew *nothing* about the robbery. It was the cashier's idea. He went to Mission Bay with Nando and the other boy the police arrested, said to go in, and he would give them the cash, and then they would split it three ways. The police would never find out, a bullet proof idea. Nando would never hurt anyone. The old man that caused the accident, his last name was Bacon, like a pig. He had a heart attack and that's when he swerved into the fire truck. Nando carried a saw, the heaviest equipment because he was physically the strongest. He was the first one out of the truck, to lead the crew when they arrived to a job. He didn't die instantly, like a lot of people believe or what was said in the news. He rose from the pavement, weary, was on one knee, trying to get up. After I identified the body, there was a ceremony for him at the camp, where he was incarcerated. A guy, who was there at the time of the accident, came up to me and said Nando tried to stand. Nando looked at him, but he really wasn't looking at him. Nando was seeing through him, like if he saw a light. Then, Nando collapsed one last time in the arms of this man. Nando fought for his life until the end, but he's gone. My baby boy is gone."

Pleasure won't feel so good without the pain and neither would happiness if it wasn't for sadness. Family can use us to uplift their broken spirits regardless of their mistakes and mishaps. We can show our family tough love and hope that they understand that they are not only hurting themselves but hurting those who care about them. We have to understand that we all had different upbringings in different environments. We all went through different experiences even though we had some similarities. Some of us obviously made better decisions than others and benefit from that. However, this doesn't mean that we look down upon those who didn't make good decisions in disgust or shame. Maybe a little disappointment but, nonetheless, we must still look upon each other as family. As family that needs our help as a person they can come and talk to, if nothing else. As someone who can help lift their hopes and spirits, even if just for a brief moment. As a family member who is concerned, who does care. We must understand we all get lost on the way to growing up. Regardless of how much or how far we are gone from walking or choosing a good path, we can always help one another to regain focus on better lifestyles and better ways of living. Believe me, there's always people out there who are doing the exact opposite. Sometimes, we can be our only saviors, but only when we are able to see the light. The light that leads to better days.

A Dream in the Sky

A dream in color or a dream in black and white? In the end, it's all the same. Nando is a little boy, the same little boy with a scar on his head, the same boy with an innocent smile full of mischief and laughter. I am on the beach, the waves crashing against the shores, with endless miles of sand surrounding me, free of footprints to lead me back in the right direction. The sun rotates into a tangy color. I try to find Nando, but he is missing. I track up and down the beach, searching, calling his name repeatedly. There is no place for me to run. I am afraid he might be dead since he abruptly disappeared, and I am left alone to watch the shadows of my imagination form a gray line of fear. From behind the cliffs, from behind the perpetual moving shores and the merciful waves, Nando appears, his face like the color of clouds, a light orange before the sunsets. Both his arms are broken, but he smiles to let me know he survived, and I cry tears of relief because in my dreams, he is alive, and in my dreams, I have the power to save him.

It was good to speak to you. You sounded very delightful. It was a good thing I decided to call Cat's house that night. Otherwise, who knows when I wouldn't have been able to talk to you. It was good to hear your voice for that brief moment. You sounded good, very joyful, as did everyone else I spoke to that night.

Good thinking on betting on the Saints. I also bet with them and won a few bucks. Nothing close to what you made, but nonetheless I won something. I'll be looking forward to come watch a Charger game at your future home or attend some kind of gathering together. I'm sure there will be many, and they all will be a blast. Too bad about your pay cut. I've seen on the news that some schools are on strike already. It also said that they are trying to work things out. I hope the bargaining works out for the better for you and your colleagues. I'll keep my fingers cross.

No doubt there will be many more obstacles ahead, some easier than others, some more challenging, difficult, and demanding, but nevertheless, with your perseverance, I'm confident you will continue to prevail and shine through any dark and trouble time that you may face. Just know that I will try my best to help you out in anyway that I can through whatever you need or want so long as you remain true to yourself and those dearest to you. Just try to remember the important things that matter in your life, for this will help you stay humble.

Coming Away

"Do you want to sign the guestbook? Over 2,000 have attended the rosary so far," the door attendant working at the funeral parlor informs me as he reaches for another guestbook from underneath the podium. The parking lot is jam-packed with vans and SUVs, with license plates from different states, headlights that shine in the night, causing traffic buildup for blocks down the street.

Mourners cram inside the chapel to view the body. A line of family, friends and more give their condolences to Uncle Chunky, who sits on the first bench in the chapel, his children in rows behind. I swindle through a crowd of adults, making my way to my uncle. I give him a tight hug before I turn to the body.

"Big V, he's waiting for you."

I slowly walk down the middle of the aisle and approach the coffin. I do not hear background noise, and I only feel my eyes burn more and more the closer we meet, the closer I am to saying goodbye. Nando is peaceful, which makes the sight even harder. The left side of his face, scraped and rough from the accident, is covered in makeup, but he is still handsome. His long hair in two braids. He is dressed in a blue suit with many handmade beaded necklaces and sage tucked away in his pocket. Photos of him, laughing with the boys, hugging the girls, eating pizza, opening Christmas gifts, are placed by his side. Baskets of heavenly white lilies decorate the room, giving it a sense of ease.

Tio Rick sings the spirits of Nando's favorite song, "Emancipate yourself from mental slavery. None but ourselves can free our minds." The comfort of Tio's voice plays in his guitar. Music made for healing on what was taken away, music that lives through life. "Have no fear for atomic energy 'cuz none of them can stop the time." This is a reggae Aztlan that will keep Nando in harmony.

After the song, I am introduced to respectfully read the first of three eulogies. Cat and Monchi asked me the day after Nando's passing to speak, and with great honor, I accepted. I recite excerpts from the letters we wrote to each other. At the end of my speech, I turn to his body, place my final letter by his side, and give him a final kiss.

The Chaplin of the fire department preaches the words of the Bible, "We cannot reverse God's order. When God says something comes first, it comes first. God has blessed Brother Nando, and brought him to the next level in faith. God has removes all of Brother Nando's sins, and Brother Nando can now see how perfect God made him. Brother Nando is given a new body, a body that does not hurt, that does not feel pain. No matter where Brother Nando has been, no matter what Brother Nando had done in the previous time in his life, he came back to a place where he can receive what God already had for him. Brother Nando is at peace with the Lord. Brother Nando now has the light of life."

Uncle Chunky follows at the end and shares a memory with the listeners, "I was driving Nando one day to summer school, and I pulled into the parking lot of the school. I asked him what class he flunked. He said English. I looked at him and said, you flunked English? You don't speak Spanish. Now, you can't speak English. What do you speak?" Uncle Chunky makes us laugh gently, makes us smile, even in his darkest time.

Yeah, my routine is tiring and a bit overwhelming at times, which is why I sometimes tend not to do the whole thing. But sometimes, I feel really good when I do the whole thing or even more than half of it. It really depends on how I'm feeling when I get up. I usually get it going, so I can do it and get it over with. Plus, it helps pass the time, and it feels good to get a good workout like that in. I got a job now, so I don't get to sleep in no more like I used to. It makes me spend all my mornings outside, with most of the afternoon. I work on the tier. Basically, I keep it clean and running errands for the tier cop.

When I was doing my training earlier this year and we were on the hiking part, we would be near Yosemite. On a couple of hikes, we would be able to see certain parts of Yosemite once we reached the top of the mountain. That's like the worst thing that can happen besides falling off the side of the mountain is running out of water and dehydrating. That's what makes our packs so heavy, all that water we carry, but the outdoors are pretty cool and awfully nice. The hikes are worth the view you get to take in. Real good scenery.

By the way, thanks for the postcard. It looks beautiful there as well as exciting. I know it was hotter than hell and a great adventure. That's cool that you went camping along to coast of Baja. I might have to put that on my to-do list. I've only been camping once, and it was a blast. That's cool that you know how to put a campsite; that comes in handy sooner or later. Argentinian and flank steak sound delicious. I bet it tastes exotic. I could even just go for a regular big, juicy steak, with a lot of good BBQ sauce. Got some little ones here but they weren't cooked right and the sauce was watered down, so it was really plain. To go snorkeling looks like fun. It's like going into a whole new world. I would like to do that someday.

Sometimes, time can be your friend, and sometimes it can be your foe. I ponder not of all the days I got left, but instead of how I can stay strong in the head. I am no longer a pawn for I am the king in my own game of chess, so it is very important that I don't get misled. I must and will always stay ready and prepared for any and everything that lies ahead.

Walking to Honor

Funerals are meant to be sad, but in this case, I am *proud*. The loud sirens of the fire trucks pass through a neighborhood of people, who stand still, take off their hats, and salute. A dozen Harley-Davidson riders, in their leather vest and dark sunglasses, rev their engines together to form a powerful roar. Double seated custom motorcycles are tied with miniature American flags on both handlebars. Lowriders with hydraulic suspension systems and custom paint jobs of an eagle and serpent on the hood follow in an organized line. TJ and Ricky come out of a crafted Chevy, both in three-piece suits. They put on their white gloves and approach the hearse. They pull the coffin from the back; Wicho and Monchi, who wear tribute t-shirts with their younger brother on the front, also assist as pallbearers. These men, once young boys, on the roof top of a house, in the streets with scraped knees, carry their leader to peace.

Firefighters dressed in their firmly pressed uniforms and clean-shaved faces stand with their hands behind their back in one single line, showing their respect to the fallen hero. Uncle Chunky and Tio Rick sing together as Tio strums his *requinto*, tears running down their faces, but their voices remain strong enough to carry out "Place in the Sun." A beautiful sight of a father singing his son to the end. An elderly lady tenderly bangs on a drum, crafted of deerskin. Esmi, in a black dress, and Cat, with red lipstick and a red flower in her hair, burn sage that surrounds the grave. An indigenous man blows in a shell horn, facing each direction of the earth, north, east, south, and west. As he puffs into the ocean jewel, everyone turns to the path and bows. The #58 Mission Bay football jersey is presented to Uncle Chunky, and my dad positions a Charger flag on top of the casket. Aunt Virgie places a single rose next to the Charger flag and hugs her brother. I take off my sunglasses and faithfully look into the hopefulness of the sky. Two hawks glide overhead, circling in sync, like dancing partners, making sure that together, they are free.

Final Letter:

Santa Clarita, October 18th 2010

It's always easy to pawn something off on another person, but it takes a strong person to own up to one's actions and correct the problem. Not everyone is capable of that or forgiveness. There are many who feel that it is better to ask for forgiveness than for permission. There are many of us who lack the power to truly forgive. Some are able to partially and momentarily forgive, always holding on and waiting for a good chance to throw it all back in your face, "Vendetta forgiveness." Many people are good at that. All in all, it comes down to one's standards and morals. For that is what plays the biggest part in forgiving. Everyone needs to practice forgiving because if you don't, all you're left with is hate. There will always be hate and there will always be war because that's what this world thrives off. It's how we were taught. Since kids, we learned to hate and create war.

That's crazy that ninety-year-old man was driving. Miraculously, he didn't die, and you came out of it uninjured. Sorry for all of the trouble you got to deal with because of the accident and the totaled truck. It's a good thing you made the sign of the cross because without it, you might have been hurt and that would have been all bad. I'm glad you weren't harmed and hope you stick with your little predriving ritual.

That's kind of crazy that you have that gift or, should I say, curse. I know I would have been in straight denial first couple of times they would have popped up. Then, I would have tried to talk to them to see what's up with them and why they're coming to check me out, but I'm crazy like that. Have you ever tried talking to them? I think you should try to muster up the courage and give it a shot. If things start to get a little crazy for you, just hurry up and start praying as fast as you can. By any chance, can you make out their facial features? I'm sure you're not the only one to experience these types of phenomena. I'll ask that the spirits come bother me rather you because I can use the company. Plus, I want to know what they're about because you don't need that added or extra worries or stress in your life. I'll pray for that, even though I don't pray. I'll do that for you, and I'll put in a prayer request asking the same.

You just stay strong, keep your faith, and pray as well. Take the going to church thing serious. Keep your devotion. Don't just go to go through the motions. Go because you want to be there. Just keep believing strongly in your higher power and be loyal. It's all about what's best for you, mentally, physically, emotionally and spiritually. That is for you to decide, not anyone else. You know your worth, so never play yourself short or let anyone else make you think differently. I hope you were able to make all your decisions clear minded and to fit your wants and needs. Just be cautious and learn from your mistakes. Don't let them remain mistakes; turn them into life lesson and educate yourself, as you would in school. Stay on top of things and don't allow things to get to a point where you're second-guessing anything. Do what you feel you need to do in order to obtain your happiness. That's good that you're going to church like that. I hope you keep attending on a regular basis. It seems your faith is getting stronger and that's good. Just make sure you stick to your beliefs. I'm glad it helps lift your spirits. What's good for the heart is good for the soul. Maybe you can get your dad to go with you sometime, after football season, of course.

As for me, though, still hanging in there. I'm at a different camp now, closer than where I was but still a little drive. We are by Six Flags Magic Mountain. It's called

Francisquito, and it's an LA county camp, which means we hike every day of the week except on weekends or if we get some kind of assignment to get out of it, which is rare but does happen on occasions. If it rains really hard, then we don't hike. Some of them are really vicious, too, and we have to make them by a certain time or else we get written up. Then, every Wednesday we have to pack hike, and I have to carry the saw. Then, the foremen, our bosses, be acting funny and having mood swings, so they'll treat us all fucked up and cracked the shit out of us. What really sucks is we don't even catch that many fires. While most of the camps get over 1,000 hours a season, our highest crew is barely over 300 hours. We get paid a dollar an hour plus our grade pay, which is like $1.45 or $1.95, depending on our job position. I'm still lifting weights, though, and getting a little stronger. My max is 325 lbs.

It was great to finally see family. It was over a year and a half since I've seen anyone. Chunk certainly is one-of-a kind, a one-man show that never seems to disappoint. Always fun to watch. Always bringing out the life in me. I'm sorry to say that my dad doesn't move as well as he used to. I was still very happy to see him, though. I miss him, along with everybody else. I'm glad this year is almost over. Only have one more to go, and then it's home sweet home.

On October 16th, 2011, Fernando Julio Sanchez was honored at the 30th Annual National Fallen Firefighters Memorial Service in Emmitsburg, Maryland.

Acknowledgements

Thank you, God, for allowing me a gift to share with the world. To my parents who provide unconditional love and presences in my life. To my nana and the rest of the Pedroza family, your support and love means the world to me. To the Sanchez clan that reaches from Blythe to San Diego to Mendota, you are a wild bunch. Aunt Virgie, Uncle Chunky, and Tio Rick, thank you for making us laugh throughout the book. Without your characters, it would have been entirely sad. To the Galindo, Navarro, Correa, Le Blanc, Nash, and Gennarelli family, you are my extended *familia*. Glory, thank you for sharing your talents with us and always supporting me through the creative process. Adie, you will always be my partner in crime. Gio, thank you for taking the time to read over the book and providing me with your honest feedback. Evie and Angelica, the sky is the limit when it comes to your writing talents. Tom and Rama, thank you for giving me the kick start I needed to begin the writing process. Brandon, thank you for the idea of including a preface. Carlos, thank you for making look like a girl. Jason, thank you for the support, tolerance, and breakfast sandwiches while I completed the book. To the men and women that fight, fought, and have died to keep the freedom of our country, I am forever grateful. To the reader, thank you for the support and understanding that comes in reading the book. You are all a part of Nando.

20649201R10072

Made in the USA
Charleston, SC
20 July 2013